# A FINE KIND OF MAD-NESS

MOUNTAIN
ADVENTURES
TALL
AND
TRUE

## LAURA & GUY WATERMAN

THE
MOUNTAINEERS
BOOKS

Published by
The Mountaineers Books
1001 SW Klickitat Way, Suite 201
Seattle, WA 98134

First printing, 2000.

Published simultaneously in Great Britain by Cordee, 3a DeMontfort Street, Leicester, England, LE1 7HD

Manufactured in the United States of America

Project Editor: Dottie Martin
Editor: Miriam Bulmer
Designer: Ani Rucki

Cover illustration: *Mountain Climber* (wood engraving), 1933, Rockwell Kent [1882–1974]
Illustrations by Rockwell Kent: page 9: *Prometheus* (engraving on copper), 1931; page 73: *Girl on Cliff* (wood engraving on maple), 1930; page 155: *Flame* (wood engraving on maple), 1928

*Library of Congress Cataloging-in-Publication Data*
Waterman, Laura.
    A fine kind of madness : mountaineering adventures, tall and true /
Laura and Guy Waterman.
        p.      cm.
    ISBN 0-89886-734-7 (pbk.)
    1. Mountaineering.  I. Waterman, Guy. II. Title.
    GV200 .W28 2000
    796.52'2—dc21
                                                        00-009642
                                                            CIP

 Printed on recycled paper

FOR CHLOE,
ECHO AND
TUCKERMAN,
BRUTUS,
KENSEY,
BAILEY,
AND JAMIE,
AND IN
MEMORY
OF
ELSA

## Other books by Laura and Guy Waterman

*Backwoods Ethics:*
*Environmental Concerns for Hikers and Campers* (1979 edition)

*Forest and Crag:*
*A History of Hiking, Trail Blazing and Adventure in the Northeast Mountains*

*Yankee Rock & Ice:*
*A History of Climbing in the Northeastern United States*

*Backwoods Ethics:*
*Environmental Issues for Hikers and Campers* (1993 edition)

*Wilderness Ethics:*
*Preserving the Spirit of Wildness*

# CONTENTS

# PREFACE

Mountains have always inspired storytelling. The classical Greek bards, brooding in the shadow of Mount Olympus, created those marvelous gods and goddesses, with all their superhuman strengths and all-too-human frailties. We haven't the slightest doubt that the Incas in the Andes, and the ancient Tibetans, and Russian peasant storytellers at the foot of the Caucasus must have told wild tales, tall and true.

For us, with our lower mountains and less elevated storytelling powers, these two worlds have been part of our lives since our earliest memories. It's hard to say which came first for us, the mountains or the writing.

Laura grew up as the daughter of Emily Dickinson's Boswell, Thomas H. Johnson, and the house was redolent with scholarship and the erudite turn of phrase. But the family summered in the New Hampshire hills where, at her bedroom window, the last thing Laura saw each evening and the first thing she saw each morning was the beckoning profile of Mount Monadnock.

In junior high, Guy lived close enough to come home for lunch. His mother would have sandwiches and milk set out, and while Guy lunched she would read aloud from Shakespeare's plays. But his earliest childhood was spent roaming a ten-acre woodlot in Connecticut, and his father took him up Mounts Chocorua and Washington at the earliest opportunity.

Years later, we met as rock climbers. We courted at the Shawangunk cliffs during the spring, summer, and fall, and at the ice gullies and snow-drenched summits of the Adirondacks in winter. We were married at the "Gunks" and spent our wedding night on a bivouac ledge two hundred feet above level ground. During the week Laura worked as an editor at New York publishing houses, winding up as associate editor of *Backpacker* magazine at its birth. Guy became a speechwriter for various moguls of the political and corporate worlds.

When we began homesteading in the wooded hills of Vermont, we divided our leisure time between climbing in New Hampshire's White Mountains and writing about mountains. The twenty stories in this collection come from that rich time of our lives.

The unifying theme in these stories is an exploration of the basic impulse to climb, and its roots in the underlying drives of remarkable individual climbers.

The first section looks closely at certain characters who stamped their distinctive personalities on the climbing scene and on their fellow climbers.

The second batch confronts danger and death in the mountains, and climbers eyeing uneasily these shadows always on the edge of their world.

The third explores the enduring mystery of why people climb, its meaning in their lives, and what we see and what we cannot see in the mountains and in the people who are drawn irretrievably to them.

About half of these stories are true; the other half-fictional inventions are rooted in the reality of our or others' climbing experiences. About one-third were written by Laura alone, one-third were written by Guy alone, and the others (most of the nonfiction) are collaborations. The nonfiction stories appeared first mainly in two of our books: *Yankee Rock & Ice: A History of Climbing in the Northeastern United States* (Stackpole Books, 1993) and *Wilderness Ethics: Preserving the Spirit of Wildness* (Countryman Press, 1993). The fiction has mostly appeared in a variety of journals, but three of the stories appear here for the first time. We are grateful to The Mountaineers Books for their professional skill in producing it. Most of all we appreciate the encouragement and guidance given by John Daniel, from the very conception of this idea to its realization. It is unquestionably true that this book would not have happened without him, and he's been such a pleasure to be involved with all along the way.

We also are thankful to have spent so many years in the community of climbers and the exalted company of mountains. These were the focus of our life for a quarter century. We've had exciting times, sometimes terrifying, more often hilarious, but always interesting, absorbing.

Whether climbing is a sport or a grim challenge, be it ballet, gymnastics, a route to wilderness or to the inner self, a romp of the spirit or a way of life that beats working—it all comes down to a metaphor for something more important than the vertical rock or ice, which is all the nonclimber sees.

These stories strive to express the impulse to climb in a variety of moods and manifestations.

*Laura and Guy Waterman*
*East Corinth, Vermont*
*January 2000*

BLAZ-
ING
THE
WAY

# Strong Personalities Leave Their Mark on the Mountains—and on Their Fellow Climbers

Serious historians frown on what they deride as the "great man" theory of history. Historical forces, they assure us, are such profound compulsions that individuals are merely actors tossed roles in the staging of great events, specks on the crests of waves churned by deep sea changes.

But what can they say about climbing? The men (mostly) and women who enact the breakthroughs in climbing standards are up there on the cutting edge, all by themselves, physically and psychologically. There's no way to dismiss them as tools of blind fate. Their will, their courage, their decisive acts, each shines as a flash of individual creation.

Writing about climbing inevitably means writing about this elect handful of individual climbers. Over the years, like most climbers, we've thought a lot about our pioneering predecessors. When you're standing on the bottom edge of a terrifying series of upward moves, you have to think about the climber who first sallied up there, not knowing what holds would materialize, whether it would "go" at all, trying to suppress consideration of consequences in event of failure. They are heroes and heroines, make no mistake.

The stories that follow mull over a half dozen or so of these pioneering climbers. We've been privileged to know some (Fritz, Robert), to climb with some (Lester, Henry), to merely hear about others (Miriam, Annie, Fanny). (For some reason, these people are all referred to by their first names. Musicians don't speak of Wolfgang and Ludwig and Johannes, but it would seem stilted to talk of Germer and Barber and Peck.)

What were they like? What did it mean to take those first appalling steps into the unknown? Who are they?

# THE BIG LITTLE MAN FROM DRESDEN

**B**ecause he was often climbing at the same cliffs we were during the 1960s and 1970s, we came to know Fritz Wiessner slightly. Of course we held him in that same awe and respect that every climber of our day did. We first wrote about him in a chapter in our history of climbing in the northeastern United States, the only chapter devoted entirely to one man. For that, we interviewed him for several hours at his home in Vermont. Later, sadly, we borrowed from that chapter to write his obituary.

A less likely physical specimen for a man who was the greatest climber of his generation can scarcely be imagined. The reader, hearing his name and reputation, pictures a tall, handsome, hawk-eyed Teuton, godlike, with a shock of wavy blond hair, broad bronzed shoulders, slender hips, and an air of Wagnerian grandeur and Nietzschean mystery about him, but in reality he would have been taken for a baker or bartender rather than a great alpinist. More gnome than god, he was well below average height, balding, slope-shouldered and stocky, almost without a waist. His features readily creased in a wide and friendly grin. The surface did not easily disclose his strength of arm or catlike agility, while that cheerful grin concealed drive and determination almost unparalleled even among the world-class climbers of his day.

**Source:** Adapted from Chapter 7 ("Fritz Wiessner") in *Yankee Rock & Ice: A History of Climbing in the Northeastern United States,* by Laura and Guy Waterman.

▲ ▼ ▲

**The fairyland world of freestanding sandstone towers and airy pinnacles near** Dresden, Germany, was where Wiessner learned what climbing meant—and what was expected of a Dresden man. At Dresden, at the dawn of the twentieth century, the pure art of free rock climbing shot ahead of standards in France, Switzerland, Italy, and England. The brilliant Fehrmann, the great bearish Oliver Perry-Smith, and others were there mastering moves up blank corners, overhanging cracks, and other great problems. The climbers at Dresden were simply the best.

Born in 1900, as a teenager Fritz moved into this world of excellence and rapidly developed the technical skills—and tapped into the inner fire—that propelled him into the front rank of world-class free climbing. By the mid-1920s he was repeating the most difficult and infrequently climbed routes throughout the Alps and doing his own first ascents at a demanding standard. His special strength lay in wide crack climbing, which requires both technical mastery and uncommon strength.

Alone of all the top German climbers, Wiessner elected to come to the United States, emigrating in 1929 and becoming an American citizen in 1935. Had others of the Dresden men come over, the course of American climbing might have been very different and more rapidly approached European standards. But since he came alone, his name and climbing achievements here during the 1930s stand in a class by themselves.

It was not until 1931 that Wiessner made contact with American climbers. At that time, a handful of New York City climbers had just begun to explore the cliffs of the Hudson River highlands fifty to seventy-five miles north of Manhattan. Fritz contacted Percy Olton, leader of these pioneers, and was invited to join them on an outing to a riverside cliff known as the Crow's Nest.

On the first day, the newcomer served notice that a new standard of free climbing was in store for the New World by attacking that most characteristic of Wiessner attractions: a wide, slanting crack. Above the strenuous start, intricate routefinding led up through delicate face-climbing, laybacks, and an overhang. The excited New York climbers dubbed this intimidating line *Fritz's Ritzy Route* and hastened to introduce the new man to all of the principal cliffs they knew. At each he established routes of a difficulty they had been unwilling to try. On Arden it was the *Piton Route,* "by far the most difficult" on the cliff (in Olton's words), surmounting steep bulges and a strenuous hand traverse. On Storm King, Fritz worked out *The Chimney,* more difficult than all earlier lines, requiring "a greater variety of climbing than any other course in the Highlands . . . and there [was] no doubt about the exposure," according to a thoroughly impressed Olton. On Breakneck Ridge, *Fritz's Prize Route* took a magnificent line up the steep, dark rock, with "the smallest margin of climbability" of any of the Hudson Highland climbs.

In 1933, impatient to find harder and higher climbs, Wiessner contacted Robert Underhill, the Harvard philosophy professor who was then the acknowledged dean of American climbers. Underhill suggested a visit to the big cliffs of the White Mountains of New Hampshire.

At Cathedral Ledge, Underhill showed Wiessner a direct start to the standard route, an awkward flaring crack that Will Allis, an Underhill protégé, had barely managed to struggle up. In today's rating system, Allis's lead would be rated 5.7, about as hard as anything yet climbed on this side of the Atlantic in 1933. Ever at home in a wide crack, Fritz went up it effortlessly. ("They did not know how to do these climbs," explained the patient veteran of the Dresden circle.) When Underhill called up that he would not attempt to follow that way, so that a complex rearrangement of ropes and belays would be necessary, Fritz called back to ask if the route went straight up through the crack. Assured that it did, Wiessner simply untied, threw down the rope, and soloed up the remaining three pitches of the *Cathedral Standard* (rated 5.6).

At Cannon, Wiessner opened a third line north of the original routes. This was the first to involve the "Old Man" profile, as it finishes by climbing a splendid corner among the various vertical planes that, seen from the road two thousand feet below, compose the famous profile. Although technically easier than either of the original two lines, Wiessner's route has become a much-traveled course, despite the risk of much loose rock. In seconding the original ascent, Underhill was impressed less with the technical skill of the lead than with Wiessner's agility in threading his way through so much loose rock and gravel without dislodging anything on his follower. "Like a cat on the rock," he marveled.

On this New Hampshire trip, Wiessner also opened up a new cliff, Humphrey's Ledge, in the neighborhood of Cathedral and Whitehorse.

While these New Hampshire triumphs were highly admired at the time, Wiessner's technical prowess reached its greatest American pitch on the unlikely ground of Connecticut's little traprock cliffs. In three years, 1933 through 1935, Fritz made several visits to the New Haven area, teaming up with the best of the local climbers there. At the Sleeping Giant he established a splendid line up the highest section of the Chin, which remained the standard of the area for years. At East Peak he swarmed up a classic Wiessner jam crack that widens into a chimney, then leads out over an overhang into a double crack system above—all unrelentingly vertical and wildly exposed, rated 5.7, although clearly harder than anything given that rating in New Hampshire or New York in 1933, and still a popular and demanding climb today under the name of *Rat Crack*.

It was at Ragged Mountain that Fritz's most imposing lines were put in. In the center of the highest cliff is a low-angle slab that rises to a broad ledge 30 feet below the top. From either side of this ledge, large vertical cracks lead straight to the top. Few holds help the climber; they must be dealt with by good jamming techniques or wide stemming. Fritz climbed both with virtually no protection and in a style that modern climbers rate 5.8. This was a level of difficulty new for the United States. Twenty years later a Yale climber said of one of these cracks, "Your author knows it exists but doesn't even want to see it, let alone you-know-what it."

Even more astonishing at the time was *Vector,* which Fritz put up with Roger Whitney in 1935. The current authority on Connecticut rock, Ken Nichols, describes *Vector* thus: "Starting as a small, relatively easy inside corner, this fine route finishes as a flared crack through a bulge. It was a bold lead in the mid-1930s, with only a single pin being placed for protection below the bulge before a 20-foot runout through the crux above." Fritz went up twice to try it but each time turned back, reluctant to commit himself to such a strenuous and unprotected sequence of moves. On the third occasion he made the commitment and completed what probably remained the hardest single lead in the country for almost twenty years.

In the late 1930s, Wiessner got to New York's Adirondacks. He had made a brief and unsatisfactory reconnaissance earlier, at which time a cursory look at Wallface left him with the impression that this largest of Adirondack cliff faces was unclimbable. After being snowed off in 1936 and 1937, he returned on Memorial Day weekend in 1938 and pushed a line up the center of the face that had repulsed earlier attempts. By this time, Wiessner had fallen in love with Wallface and its setting, which he ever after regarded as the most beautiful climbing area in the Northeast, because of the "feeling of altitude" and the "charm of solitude" so uniquely combined there. During that three-day weekend in 1938, Fritz and his party also polished off new routes on Indian Head and at Chapel Pond, advancing the standard of difficulty at each cliff.

An oft-told legend of American rock climbing concerns that brilliantly clear moment following an afternoon thundershower when Fritz and his party topped out on Breakneck Ridge above the Hudson River, gazed off to the northwest, and saw . . . the future of northeastern rock climbing. As a long, low line of sparkling white cliffs glittering on the horizon, the Shawangunks beckoned. Fritz was up there the following weekend and led the first routes on these cliffs, which became the principal arena for northeastern rock climbers throughout the 1940s, 1950s, and 1960s, and remain among the most popular and important climbing scenes in the United States today.

It was not long before Fritz and his New York friends realized that the venerable old Mountain House, one of those grand nineteenth-century mountain resorts still operating, rich in antiquarian ambiance, was situated squarely amidst miles and miles of climbable Shawangunk conglomerate. An enchanted setting for their favorite pastime! Directly across Mohonk Lake from that resort, up a small wooded talus slope, were beautiful, clean, solid cliffs. That first summer, 1935, Fritz headed up that talus slope and, with characteristic bold ambition, picked a perfectly dead-vertical line up a broken crack (of course: always a crack for Fritz) squarely in the most exposed and dramatic location. From the top of this route, a rope can hang more than one hundred vertical feet without touching the cliff at its base, so steep is the line. It was an elegant line, a worthy inauguration for "Gunks" climbing. A projecting slug of rock near the top gave the route its name: *The Gargoyle*. It is rated 5.5 today.

Wiessner was instantly aware that the Shawangunks were a superior arena for technical rock climbing. Not even Fritz could foresee, however, that this was to become the center of eastern climbing for years.

In 1940 a second European climber arrived on the Shawangunks scene. Born in Trieste, Hans Kraus had been tutored as a child by James Joyce, received a medical education in Vienna, and turned to sports medicine as his area of specialization, a field in which he rose to prominence as a doctor, author, and proponent of physical fitness. He moved to America in 1938, accepting a position on the staff of the prestigious Columbia Presbyterian Medical Center. His fame was enhanced when he played a role in establishing the President's Council on Physical Fitness, and he later numbered President Kennedy among his back patients.

But throughout his long career on two continents, the short, barrel-chested, athletic Dr. Kraus pursued an avocation with equal determination and flair: rock climbing. Having sharpened his skills on the vertical towers of the Dolomites, he eagerly took to the Shawangunks' verticality when he moved to the United States.

Kraus and Wiessner became the "Hans and Fritz" of American rock climbing. They single-handedly opened the Gunks wide. Of fifty-eight multi-pitch routes known to have been put up before 1950, all but two had either Hans or Fritz on the first-ascent party, and seven had them both. In those pioneering years they picked off the true classic lines of the Gunks, climbs that still rate among the most beautiful and enjoyable in the Northeast. Most of their best fell in the 5.5 to 5.6 range: Fritz's *Baby* and *Layback,* both in 1941, and *Yellow Ridge* (1944); Hans's vertical, airy *Madame Grunnebaum's Wulst* (1943); and their great collaborations, including *The Horseman* (1941), *Updraft* (1944), and the finest of all, the fittingly named *High Exposure* (1941).

Besides their outstanding 5.5 to 5.6 routes, Kraus and Wiessner also put up some of the most popular beginner routes. No other climbing area abounds in so many multi-pitch climbs of high quality on which a beginner can feel comfortable. The pure pleasure that hundreds, probably thousands, of novice climbers have gained from half a dozen of Hans's and Fritz's Shawangunk 5.2s defies measurement.

The relationship between these two expatriates was at first a friendly rivalry—Hans putting up a route one week, Fritz hearing about it and putting up another the next—but it ultimately deepened into a friendship that lasted almost half a century. As late as the 1970s, one of the privileges of climbing at the Gunks was the sight of the two small, gnomelike figures side by side on the carriage road below the cliffs, walking slowly, often with heads bowed and hands behind their backs, like two ancient dwarves from a Tolkien land, heading off for another classic Shawangunk climb, usually on a route that one or the other or both had put in three decades before.

While Fritz himself felt that his rock-climbing peak was reached in Europe during the 1920s, he emerged as a major mountaineer on the world stage during the 1930s. The catalog of his accomplishments during that decade is without equal among his contemporaries: a major attempt on Nanga Parbat in 1932; coming very, very close to climbing K2 in 1939, years before any of the big Himalayan 8000-meter peaks had been climbed; British Columbia's Waddington in 1936 with Bill House, one of the top ascents of the decade; a bold and virtually unprotected lead of Wyoming's Devils Tower, its first free ascent, in 1937, in which Fritz felt he was in top form; plus innumerable other mountaineering coups around the globe. It has been said that half the mountain ranges of the world have a "Wiessner Crack." He was called the greatest climber of his generation.

Even more astonishing, perhaps, was the incredible staying power of this Dresden youth who began climbing in 1911. When he was still getting up all his old routes at the age of sixty, younger men thought him remarkable. At sixty-four he spearheaded an attempt on the unclimbed Elephant's Head cliff in Vermont's Smugglers Notch; the first complete ascent fell to another, but not until Fritz had worked out the technical difficulties of the first pitch—a steep crack, of course. In his seventies he was still going strong, befriending young climbers, never dwelling on the past, always looking for the next climb. When nearly eighty he would apologize that he no longer cared to lead above 5.6 but would willingly follow 5.9.

Once, at the Shawangunks, when he was well over seventy, he joined a young partner to climb *Madame Grunnebaum's Wulst,* a dead-vertical 5.6 of fearsome exposure, especially on the airy second pitch. On their way to the climb, his young friend disclosed that he had recently soloed this route, at which Wiessner beamed and commented, "Ah, you must vee climbing pretty goot!" The younger man led the first pitch, then handed the rack to old Fritz, who proceeded to lead the entire second pitch, with its three wildly exposed 5.6 bulges, without placing a single piece of protection—virtually the equivalent of soloing the upper pitch. When his partner reached the top, Fritz grinned impishly and said: "I must vee climbing pretty goot!"

In his middle eighties, to observe his countenance, the spring in his step, the animation in his conversation—to say nothing of his grace on steep rock or his effervescent enthusiasm for climbing every month of the year—one might have easily mistaken him for a man in his fifties, though in unusual physical shape and with a confident attitude toward life and climbing. Finally, in his upper eighties, a series of strokes brought this remarkable climbing career to a close. Unable to climb, he had no reason to hang around any longer. He died in 1988.

In his prime, Wiessner's personal style was not universally admired. Perhaps as tacit acknowledgment of his superior skill, he insisted on leading almost every climb he did in this country during the 1930s. Underhill recalled that one of the conditions that Fritz laid down in arranging for their tour of New Hampshire cliffs in 1933 was that Fritz would do all the leading. Some other climbers found this attitude overbearing and preferred not to climb with him.

It would be incorrect to exaggerate the extent of this feeling among climbers, however. Many partners thoroughly enjoyed Wiessner's company, felt he was a patient teacher, and commented on his freedom from overbearing self-importance.

Perhaps it was merely that Wiessner recognized that only the leader undertook the genuine risk in climbing under prewar conditions, with those old hemp ropes that never would have held a long leader fall. When he was over eighty, he followed a younger climber, Jim McCarthy, up the infamous *High Exposure*. It happened that we were at the cliffs that weekend. When we saw Fritz come down, we congratulated him on climbing this celebrated route. He put off our compliments with this revealing demur: "I didn't climb it. Jim climbed it. I just followed." Then, as fifty years earlier, the old Dresden warrior felt that if you weren't out there at the sharp end of the rope, you weren't really climbing.

Although Fritz was an inspiration to modern climbers, his impact on the 1930s scene is harder to evaluate. In a sense, Fritz Wiessner was not an important influence on American climbing in the 1930s, because what he was doing was so far ahead of what others were willing to try that he did not significantly improve the general standard. His influence was felt in his dedication to Dresden ideals of free climbing, so that an entire generation of American climbers was indoctrinated with the principle that to use aid was to cheat. Furthermore, of course, he left a legacy of routes for all to enjoy. Perhaps his greatest single gift to all of us was his "discovery" of the Shawangunks.

Worldwide, he was a colossus. Reinhold Messner, the automatic choice of many as the greatest climber of the century, declines that title. To him, Wiessner was "the most important mountaineer of the twentieth century." For fifty years—half of that century!—the little man from Dresden was that big.

# THE LIONESS AT DUSK

## A STORY

by Laura Waterman

We never met Miriam O'Brien Underhill, widely regarded as the greatest woman climber of her generation (the 1920s and 1930s). Had we met her in her final years, it would have been difficult, as her brilliant mind broke long before her strong body was ready to give up. After her death, we did meet her husband, Robert L. M. Underhill, equally renowned and by then as ancient as some Old Testament patriarch. Robert and Miriam were among the handful of early-twentieth-century Americans who learned alpinism in the sport's nineteenth-century European tradition. Robert introduced European climbing techniques to North America. Miriam set the standard for daring "manless" ascents, most notably her climb of the Grépon with Alice Demesme in 1929.

Robert granted us two extended interviews; we stayed in his guest house and spent the better parts of two days on each occasion. The first was for a profile of Miriam as

"America's Greatest Woman Climber," which Laura published in *New England Outdoors* in November 1978. The second was in connection with our northeastern U.S. climbing history, *Yankee Rock & Ice*. We felt lucky to have secured these interviews not long before Robert's death.

During the later stages of Miriam's illness, Robert took her to Europe one last time, accompanied by their friend and hiking companion Louise Baldwin. We do not know if their trip included a return to the Alps, scene of Miriam's stunning climbing feats as a young woman, but the vision of such a return to the mountains, of her glory days, set against the pathos of her mental deterioration, haunted Laura until it produced this fictional account.

▲ ▼ ▲

**"She's gone. Miriam's gone!" Robert shouted, struggling to sit, groping at the spot** where his wife had been sleeping beside him on the platform that held thirty other climbers, most of them positioned head to toe.

The alpine hut smelled of stale sweat and the musty odor of too many bodies breathing in the same unventilated room.

"What? Miriam? Where?" Their friend Louise lurched out of sleep, turning in her blanket toward Robert's voice, shoving her hand against the darkness. The place between them was empty. Her fingers collided with the clammy blanket. Louise heard him begin to laugh. "Robert?" she said. "Are you all right?"

He kept laughing.

She needn't have asked that. She'd never seen Robert L. M. Underhill not up to any situation. But he *was* seventy-five.

"What do you bet she's headed for the Grépon. She's given us the slip, Louise." Robert threw off his blanket and stared straight ahead, out the window toward the invisible peaks, hands on the worn knees of his knickers. "She knows where she is, all right. We needn't have been concerned on that score. Pack up, Louise, we have to get her."

*"Silence, s'il vous plait,"* the hut guardian called out.

"Damn! I'm missing a boot." Robert was shining his flashlight.

*Monsieur*! You are waking everyone up." The guardian switched to English. He stood, fist on hips, in front of this old man who was causing him problems. "You make a little walk up the Mer de Glace today, *oui, Monsieur?* That is all? No big mountain climbing?"

*Do you know who you are talking to?* Louise thought. She wanted to shake this fellow.

"Go back to bed. It is only 1:15," the Guardian said. "I will call you when it is time."

"Guardian, you are going to have to lend me a boot," Robert said in French. "You must keep more than one pair for yourself, or do the guides keep extra pairs at the hut?" He was sitting on the end of the sleeping platform, buttoning his wool shirt with the frayed cuffs.

The guardian ran both hands through his hair, standing it in stiff spikes.

"Shaddup, old man," a climber shouted in English.

"Go back to sleep. You had a nightmare," another muttered.

Louise caught flashes of their Lycra climbing suits gleaming like tuxedo cloth in the beam of Robert's flashlight. She wanted to shout back, "This man did guideless ascents all over the Alps before you were born. Ever climbed the North Face of the Grand Teton? *He* made the first ascent. Why, Robert Underhill introduced roped climbing to North America!" But she knew such an outburst would only embarrass Robert. She knew, too, that by today's standards Robert's old routes were considered easy, and as for the guideless bit, probably everyone in the hut was climbing without a guide. Only rich tourists who climbed once a year employed guides these days.

"My wife has left already," Robert explained, looking up at the guardian and speaking as he would to a student who had waited after class to ask him a question. "She knows the route, but she isn't well and it has been some years. In fact," he waved a hand into the darkness, "this hut had not yet been built. My boots are size 11, if you can assist."

Robert stood up, a little lopsided with one boot and one stockinged foot, but Louise saw he equaled the guardian in height. He reached for his rope, a faded coil that might have come from an old rowboat. He'd been using it for a pillow during the night.

"Is that *hemp?*" the guardian asked. His hand shot out and pinched the strands.

Every climber in the hut was awake now, leaning on elbows, sitting up.

"Heavens no, man," Robert said. "Hemp went out after World War II. Now hurry, please, we must catch up with my wife."

▲  ▼  ▲

Earlier, in the stuffy hut, Miriam lay wrapped in her blanket next to the dear man who always kept himself beside her. She'd been sleeping, but she awoke with a jolt as if touched by a live match. Starlight flashed in the window like lightning. The hair on her head rose, and she remembered the electrical storm that had engulfed her and the two guides as they descended the great slabs, about to start the seventh of twelve rope-offs. When the icy rain hit, her whole body clenched in a fit of shivering. The emergency of the storm had forced her out of the role of pampered tourist. The guides gave her the job of managing the slippery ropes and keeping them from tangling. When her gloves became sodden she'd ripped them off and worked with bare hands. After that, she was on her way to becoming a real climber.

This old memory made her want to laugh. She pressed her fists to her mouth, gazing out toward the mountains. Then she studied the man asleep by her side. In the pale light his lean, lined face was the color of wax. She lifted her hand to touch his brow, then pulled back. Instead, she raked her fingers across her own forehead. Examined the tips, holding them close to her eyes.

The woman, her friend on her other side, slept on too. But she'd thrown off her blanket and lay on her back in her knickers and matching tweed jacket. Miriam reached down and pulled up the blanket, just as her friend had done for her on the flight—tucked a corner of the airline blanket around Miriam's knees and said, "Wouldn't we have been glad for *this* on Elephant Mountain?"

"Alice!"

"I'm Louise," Louise said. "Who is Alice, Miriam?"

"She probably means Alice Demesme," Robert answered. "She was Miriam's climbing partner on the Grépon." He turned toward his wife. "We're taking you back to the Alps, dear, so you can see your old routes again."

"Mountains!" Miriam clapped her hands.

"Remember our unplanned wet night out on Elephant Mountain, Miriam?" Louise said. She touched the blanket. "We both lay on the ground, back to back, curled in our raincoats."

Miriam wriggled in her seat.

"But it was worth it for that summit!" Louise went on. "Remember, Miriam? The evergreens were so thick at the top we had to push through on hands and knees. You led the way. Well, crawled!"

The two on either side of her were laughing, their moon faces bobbing, making Miriam feel she wasn't quite getting the joke. So she turned her gaze to the headrest of the seat in front, which began to go gauzy. She put out her hands, pushing in that rough way she'd parted the stumpy firs going up Elephant.

"Miriam, dear, you'll jostle the person in front," Robert said, pulling back her hands, imprisoning them between his own.

"Fog. Sun." She began to thrash against the seat belt.

"What about fog and sun, Miriam?" he asked.

She kept fighting for her hands so she could show him. *I promise you, if we climb high enough, we will land in sunlight.* But she couldn't turn it into words. Instead, she watched the back of the seat grow hard. Soon it would be impossible to bash through without breaking her fist. She wrestled harder for her hands.

"Easy, dear heart." His eyes were on her face.

If she could only reach the sunny spot, the fog would lift and she'd be—fine! She tried to tell him this in the carrying voice she'd used on their climbs when the wind was high: "Arraugarruugarrruuuga," she shouted.

"I can't understand that, Miriam," he said. "And keep your voice down, please."

She drew in a breath that felt the size of a hurricane, formed her mind, her mouth, her lips. *"Push."* There! She said it, all of it, with one word.

"Can you see what's going on in her head?" Robert leaned across his wife and said this to Louise.

"Me? If you can't, Robert, I surely can't."

The starlight zigzagged into the hut and glided across Miriam's blanket. She focused on the sleeping man, slitting her eyes. The night light bleached his mouth to a thin white line. The sight made her reach for her boots at the end of the sleeping platform. At home, when his mouth thinned like that, his voice got rough as sandpaper, and his arms tried to keep her from rushing outside. But when it was snowing or blowing, the big yellow house became stifling and she had to tear out into the storm, down their hill that led to the black highway, fly across that obstacle and land in the woods on the other side where the paths led straight up to the stunted trees and lichen-covered rocks. Here, in the high wild air, she felt more herself. Even in her bathrobe.

A brightness sliced across her mind, like a chink of light finding its way between old boards of an attic room. It made her squint with the effort to break through into the clear.

One time. Not this hut. The one lower down the mountain. She glanced down at Louise. No. Not that woman. The French girl. After supper, in the fading light, she and the round-faced French girl scouted the route they would walk while it was dark. It led up across the grassy alpland to the rocky moraine, then to the glacier and their peak. With a guide you never thought about this, scouting the part you would walk in the dark. But two women alone, why, you could get twisted around just leaving the hut. *Quel embarras!* Even two men could, without a guide. She and the French girl always thought of everything. Like taking only one rope. The guides lugged two, one for climbing and a lighter one for roping off. But to save weight, they took only one. The guidebook. She had ripped out the page with the route description and tucked it in her pocket.

Miriam shivered in the cold air of the hut and patted the pocket of her climbing suit. She smiled down at Louise, then frowned and drew her hand across her forehead. Closed her eyes and saw the round-faced French girl coming toward her in the darkness.

Their male climbing friends had laughed—not outright. They were too courteous. Behind hands. But she and the French girl caught the knowing looks.

"So, it's the Grépon via the *Mummery Crack,* is it?" One of the men said. "Let me tell you, climbers have fallen out of that crack, but no leader has fallen from near the top and lived." He swayed toward them, jigging his eyebrow.

They climbed the crack, *deux seules,* anyway.

Well, hardly alone!

They attracted quite a gallery, as every man heading for the Grépon that day stuck around to watch.

"Are you up the *Mummery Crack,* girls?" shouted the men who were with their guides on a nearby route but could not see for the mist.

"Almost," they sang out, though they had not yet reached its base.

That evening, back in Chamonix, one of the men said, "Today, the Grépon disappeared. Oh, there are still some rocks standing, but as a climb it no longer exists." He drained his wine and thumped his empty glass on the table.

"Right you are," said another. "Now that it has been done by two women alone, no self-respecting man can undertake it. A pity, too, because it used to be a very good climb."

She and the French girl laughed, but they weren't looking at the men. They were looking at each other.

The starlight clamored at the window. In the dark hut Miriam reached for what to bring, stuffing it in her pack. She brushed aside what to leave for the other two. Lifting the latch, she left the hut without a sound.

Outside, the cold hit her like a current, nipping her face, her hands. It made her open her arms. She picked out her ice ax from among the many resting against the stone wall of the hut. Hunched her shoulders to settle her pack. A lump dug into her back and she wriggled to shift it as she began walking in the direction of her peak. She knew the way: hadn't she and Alice scouted it out after supper?

The rocks of the moraine made a grinding sound under her boots, and there was a cold smell coming off the glacier. She planted her ice ax with each stride, on her way to climbing free of this groggy nightmare that sucked away names and tangled her thoughts. She could feel her face, grinning.

There! That rocky promontory emerging from the lower end of the glacier, its fang outlined against the night sky. The old breakfast spot! Where climbers stopped to munch cheese and bread, swill down tea before continuing on up the glacier toward the routes. The rough granite glinted in the starlight, cold and sharp-edged, making her fingers twitch. Her vision telescoped, picking out the cracks. Her breath loosened. She was right on schedule. It would be dawn when she reached the breakfast rock.

She spun in her tracks, looking back, but saw no one. Wheeled again in a dance of circles, her boots clattering on the rocks, flinging her arms to the sky. The lump in her pack dug into her back, but she hitched her shoulders and picked up the pace, shouting, laughing, playing the echo game with the high rock walls ahead.

▲ ▼ ▲

"Good lord, I hear Miriam," Robert said. He stopped, turning to Louise. Even though the air was cold, his forehead felt damp with sweat.

"We'll never catch up," Louise said. She was panting and leaned over her ice ax.

"She gave us the slip good and proper." Robert blew his nose, which was running in the cold.

"On the walk up yesterday, it was almost like being with the old Miriam again," Louise said.

"In a way. But when I talked about the Grépon, she gave me that blank look."

"But the way she was acting, waving her ice ax at the mountains, she seemed so happy, Robert."

"I was hoping that bringing her back to the scene of her youthful triumphs might jog her mind a bit. But I wasn't counting on her running off!"

"And a fine help I was, sleeping right through it," Louise laughed. "But I never could keep up with Miriam in the mountains, anyway. She always had to stop at trail junctions and wait for me."

"She hated to be outhiked," Robert said.

"She wouldn't start up the crack without a rope, Robert. Would she?"

"I didn't bring her here to *climb* it." He was walking again—not slow, but not fast—a mountaineer's pace that even at their ages they could keep up all day.

"Would she?" Louise asked again.

He looked over his shoulder. "She shouldn't be leading it, of course, though I bet she still could. The thing is, I certainly don't want to follow it. Right from the start you feel like that damn crack is going to spit you out. It's so steep, overhanging really, a terrible strain on the arms. It makes my hands sweat to think of it."

"Surely Miriam wouldn't attempt *that* by herself!"

"God knows."

▲  ▼  ▲

At the breakfast spot Miriam walked around to the uphill side of the fang and unslung her pack.

In the gray dawn she would pick out the route up the glacier. The last lap before the peak was where the real climbing began. She knew her timing was perfect because of the quality of the light.

She settled herself with her back to the rock, rummaged in her pack, and pulled out a boot. She turned it over in her hands. Set it beside her, and dug through her pack, turning it upside down and shaking it.

"Well, Alice, it seems I've misplaced our breakfast," she said to the air at her right.

"Then, we'll eat the boot, Miriam!" Alice's voice moved in her head, speaking in French.

"We can't do that."

"And why not?" Alice said. "If we were shipwrecked sailors we'd chew on a boot like that for days. Lots of nourishment in a good boot."

"It's Bob's boot," Miriam said, and this made them both laugh.

"What's in your pack, Alice? We'll move on to lunch."

No answer.

She sprang up. "Alice! Wait for me!" She began to lope up the glacier, her long limbs punching the air. Stopped dead, swirled and raced back to the rock, scooped up her ice ax, and hurtled off again.

▲ ▼ ▲

"Why, here's my boot!" Robert bent down to unlace the one loaned him by the guardian.

"Here's her pack. But it's empty," Louise said. "I'm beginning to see why you have such a time with her at home."

"Well, it's not so bad. She only runs in one direction, toward the mountains. I don't mind, really, except when she takes off down our hill in her bathrobe on stormy below-zero mornings. I'm getting too old for that game, Louise."

"You're very patient with her, Robert."

"I couldn't be doing this trip without you."

"Sure you could, except for the ladies' loo."

"Perhaps we should have all stayed down in Chamonix," Robert mused, as they started walking again. "But you know what? I was curious to see this new hut. Starting from so high up takes hours off the way we had to do the climb. Then, Miriam always said she never felt fully alive until she got above ten thousand feet. Look! That's the Grépon ridge, Louise." He pointed with his ice ax. "See those rock spires? Five—the sixth is hidden. That's the famous traverse between the Grépon and the Charmoz." He paused, breathing hard. "I have to stop. I can't walk uphill and talk at the same time the way I used to. But see! It's like an aerial steeplechase with a fifteen-hundred-foot drop to the west and a five-thousand-foot drop to the east, all the way down to the Mer de Glace. Miriam took to that kind of exposure like a goshawk."

"Is *that* the *Mummery Crack,* Robert?"

"It sure is! See, even at the start, you're hanging out over a thousand feet of air. The exposure's frightening and there's a formidable urge to thrust oneself deep into the crack, but the damn thing is easier to climb if you insert hand and foot only a short distance. Miriam always said the key to climbing the *Mummery Crack* was complete relaxation. But I'm wasting time standing here talking. We have to go on."

▲ ▼ ▲

Miriam pushed to walk faster; she felt her heart pumping, the valves opening like starting gates at the racetrack, releasing the red blood.

The sun crested the ridge to the east and the glacier pooled with light.

She raised her left hand, slitting her fingers over her eyes to cut the glare. When that hand got bored she switched her ice ax and used her right hand. Alice was ahead with the glacier goggles and hats. But she didn't want a hat, anyway. The sun was worming through the top of her head and into her brain. She could feel it sopping up the fog like a sponge. She wet her lips, which were beginning to burn. If her lips were burning, her head must be drying out on the inside, too. Wheeling, she stared back down the glacier, shading her eyes. Two people. Following her track. She turned and began to move up the glacier at a trot, even though those people were too far behind to beat her to the crack. Miriam flapped her arms in slow motion and sprang from right foot to left, like a mountain goat, a gazelle, an eagle.

By the time she reached the bergschrund the two behind had vanished.

There was Alice! Sitting in the niche at the base of the *Mummery Crack,* blending into the rocks. It was hard to pick her out, but Alice had the rope and was waiting.

*"Mountain goat,"* Miriam sang out, and leaped the gap between the glacier and the rocks that formed the beginning of the real climbing. Then she worked her way left along the wall of rock, the ground dropping below her until there was just air. She moved with the balance of a cat, selecting the

best of the small holds, pausing once or twice to suck in breath and let it out evenly. She imagined a fierce bird with the wingspan of an albatross, claws that clung like vise grips.

Reaching the broken-up rocks at the base of the crack, she saw Alice stand up and motion for her to sit where she could brace her legs against the solid rock and manage the rope. Alice had uncoiled it and was already tied on to the top end. Miriam picked up the bottom and knotted it around her waist. Alice gave her the thumbs-up signal and grinned. Then she started climbing.

▲ ▼ ▲

"My God," Robert whispered. He was standing with Louise on the glacier, just before it steepened to form the bergschrund.

"What's she doing, Robert?" Louise kept her voice low.

"The way she's moving her hands, I'd say she was feeding out rope. She's keeping her eyes on the crack, then looking down at her feet where the coil of rope would be to make sure it runs smoothly. She's belaying!"

They gazed in silence, watching Miriam's hands move in a sliding motion, paying out rope. Her head bent further and further back, as if watching a climber moving up the crack.

"This is awful!" Louise whispered. "How are we going to get her back?"

Just then Miriam called up the cliff, "Off belay, Alice!" She stood up and moved to slot her right fist into the *Mummery Crack.* "Climbing!" she shouted.

"Miriam, dear!" Robert waved his arms.

She turned at the sound of her name. "What style, eh?" she called down in French to the gallery below, gesturing with her chin up toward Alice.

"Miriam, please, come down," Robert called.

She turned from him and wedged her right foot in the crack and stood up on it, than slotted her fist higher. Now most of her weight was on her arm. She swiveled her body to look down. "You may start. By the time you get here, I'll be up the crack." Again she spoke in French.

"What sangfroid," Robert said to Louise. "But she doesn't know it's us."

"Robert, can't you keep her from going higher?"

He shrugged, looking at Louise, then up at his wife, his long arms lank at his sides.

"Call to her again, Robert, *please.*"

"Miriam, it's me," Robert said, but he could hardly lift his voice above a whisper.

"And Louise," Louise shouted.

Miriam hung from her fist and turned her head to face the spectators below.

"Miriam, come back," Robert shouted, but the words seemed to crack in his throat.

"Bob!" Miriam's voice rang out.

"My God, she said my name." His legs buckled and he knelt down in the snow, staring up at his wife.

"Don't you want me to climb?" She was still hanging on her fist.

"Of course. That's why we brought you here. But not the *Mummery Crack,* Miriam. Not today."

"But Alice is up there. She has me on belay." Miriam turned back to the crack.

"Miriam. Wait!"

"What for?"

"It's going to rain."

"The sky is perfectly blue. You're being an old fussy, Bob."

"There's nobody up there."

"What?"

"Alice isn't up there." He spaced out his words, making each one distinct.

Miriam looked toward the top of the crack. "Can't you see her head?"

"No. And neither can you. It's a trick of the rocks that makes you think it's a head."

She laughed.

"Like the Old Man of the Mountain," Louise shouted. "Back home."

Miriam kept on looking up, craning her neck back. Her nose and chin jutted in profiled relief against the sky.

"She can't hang there forever," Louise said.

"She'll give herself a goddamn stiff neck."

"Look, her lips are moving. But I can't hear her. What is she doing now, Robert?"

"Hell. Talking to the mountain for all I know." He had turned and was sitting now, facing out over the glacier. His elbows were on his knees, his chin sunk in his hands. "She's out of my reach. There really isn't much I can do for her now."

"She's coming down, Robert. She's climbing down the crack."

"I can't watch."

"She's doing it."

"That crack is goddamn steep."

"Now she's working her way along the rock wall. I never saw her lead the crack. She did those all-women ascents before I met her. But I'd heard about them. Every climber had. It was pioneering stuff!" Louise said.

Robert looked up at Louise. "I think she could still lead any of her old routes, even the Matterhorn. It makes me feel like such an old man."

"We're all old, now, dear," Miriam said. She was standing beside him. Her hand settled on his shoulder.

He gazed up into her face. "You're so sunburned, Miriam. Where's your hat?"

"Alice had the glacier goggles and the hats." Her eyes were wild. Her iron-gray hair frizzed out around her face as though she had been struck by lightning.

"Is that who you were talking to?"

"Yes, I told her to go on. She looked at Louise. "But there you are, Alice!" Miriam gazed back up at the crack again. She rubbed her forehead with her hand. "Alice?" she asked.

"I'm not your climbing partner from those faraway days, Miriam," Louise said. She reached out and touched Miriam's sleeve.

"Alice?" Miriam asked again.

"I'm Louise, Miriam."

She nodded, then shook her head as if trying to clear it. She brushed the back of her hand across her eyes.

Robert pushed himself up and dusted off the seat of his knickers, wet from snow. "I should have sat on my rope," he muttered to himself. Then he took her hand.

She turned, tugging at him, her face brightening. Since there was nothing left to do but hold on, he followed, and the two of them began bounding, leaping like children down the glacier.

# THE LAST ACT OF A GENTLE- MAN

**L**ester Germer took Laura on her second-ever climb. As a familiar figure around the cliffs where we climbed, Lester was an eccentric and distinctive personality and a warm friend, and both of us climbed with him from time to time over the years. Of course we heard all the gossip and rumors that pursued his long and eventful life, and were never certain that we sorted out fact from fancy. As related in this story, we were at the cliffs on that Sunday afternoon when he died.

Lester Germer was many things in seventy-five years. He was one of Bell Labs' top physicists. He was an expert on mushrooms. He knew enough about ants to publish an authoritative (and witty) treatise about them. He was president of the American Crystallographic Association, whatever that is. He won scientific awards too numerous to mention.

He very nearly won a Nobel Prize when he and a colleague discovered something important having to do with the electron microscope. (The colleague did cop the Nobel Prize in physics in 1937; Lester quietly went back to his lab, his mushrooms, and a vigorous outdoor life on weekends.) It was rumored that he had been a World War I fighter pilot, winning a citation from General Pershing, and those of us who knew him in rock climbing circles never doubted that he had personally shot down the Red Baron.

**Source:** Originally written for the New York chapter of the Appalachian Mountain Club, which published it first in the January/February 1987 issue of their newsletter, *Appie News,* and later as part of a brochure commemorating the chapter's seventy-fifth anniversary. Substantially similar material went into part of our book *Yankee Rock & Ice.*

▲ ▼ ▲

**For the last twenty-six years of his life, and to an entire generation of Hudson River** Valley rock climbers, Lester Germer was a rock climber.

At the age of forty-nine, this affable genius launched a side interest in rock climbing and was soon scaling cliffs all over the Northeast with whoever would join him. As his professional career wound down, his interest in climbing loomed larger. After partial retirement—he never really retired, but moved from Bell to the faculty of Cornell in deference to corporate customs promulgated for lesser mortals—he became a weekend fixture at the Shawangunk cliffs, in the Hudson River Valley. By the end of the 1960s, he was probably the most widely known and best-loved individual in the community of rock-climbing regulars there. Tall, spare, white-haired, bespectacled Lester was a gentle, genial gentleman at all times. Soft-spoken and quick with a smile and a twinkle in his eye, he was the friend of everyone from beginners to the best climbers of the day.

Lester began climbing during a conservative era of extreme safety-consciousness, and his casual enthusiasm and willingness to try anything with anybody were frowned upon by the official club leadership. For many years, the Qualifications Committee sternly refused to certify him as leader, once passing him over with the notation in the minutes: "Not passed. Likes people too much and is too enthusiastic." Yet Lester continued to show up at the cliffs and climb what he pleased with whom he pleased. "Lester Germer," mused one club leader of the 1950s, "is past reforming." The club changed before Lester did: by the 1960s, most of the old conservative rules had been relaxed, as it became clear that Lester's more casual climbing style was being widely adopted by others without any alarming rash of accidents. By the end of the 1960s, Lester was over seventy years old and doing less difficult climbs than he had in his "youth," when he was a buoyant sixty or sixty-five. But his enthusiasm for vertical rock was undimmed and his love for people greater than ever. So he settled into a weekend routine of leading novice climbers up anything they'd like, up to a standard of about 5.5.

At that time there was an excellent beginner's weekend each season and a superb network of established climbers for the rest of the year, but a gap in between, so that intermediate climbers, still reluctant to lead, sometimes had trouble finding people to climb with. Lester was their man. He alone was always ready to lead intermediate-level climbs with patience and joy. He became a "one-man climbing school," in the words of one climber of those years.

The number of individuals who basked in the companionship and encouragement and fun of climbing with old Lester during those years defies calculation. Some of us still wondered about his safety procedures and his venerable fluffy white climbing rope (which really should have been retired), but Lester had never taken even one leader fall in a quarter century of climbing, and we personally saw several occasions when that fluffy old rope, and the crinkly old hands that held it, caught follower falls with assurance and skill.

We recall once climbing *RMC,* a popular 5.5 climb, with Lester sometime around 1970. Lester wandered up that cliff with the same air of bemused abstraction other seventy-four-year-olds might have as they shuffled across a city park, talking half to himself, half to us, repeating old stories, chuckling and beaming. Except this was no city park, but a thin, vertical rock face 150 feet above the fractured boulders below. It was, as always, a treasured experience.

In the first weekend of October 1971, Lester was, as usual, at the cliffs, leading fortunate intermediates up his favorite routes. It was a beautiful fall weekend, and Lester led climbs both days, all day. Toward the end of Sunday afternoon, we heard that Lester would turn seventy-five in one week, which meant that he had the same birthday as Laura. "Lester," she said to him as he prepared to take one more party up *Double Chin,* "I was born on October 10, too!"

"Yes," he replied with a well-worn twinkle in his eye, "but what century?" Proud of his age and defying Father Time, Lester headed off for his last climb.

On the first pitch was one of those big overhangs for which those cliffs are infamous. Lester started up, then hesitated, came down, and sat on a ledge for a couple of minutes, without explanation. Perhaps he had a premonition. If so, he decided that there would be no better fate, so again he launched himself at that monster ceiling.

Technically, it is fair to say he never took a leader fall in his life. The coroner told us the next day that the heart attack was so sudden and so massive that he must have been dead before the rope held by his second came tight.

Lester's death was as considerate and helpful to everyone as his life had been. He died at the very end of a beautiful weekend, so that no one missed a climb. He chose the first pitch of a climb near the road, so there was no difficulty in bringing the body down. He was, of course, taking a large party of intermediates up a route they would find challenging, but—inspired by his cajolery—feasible and exhilarating.

When the news spread, there was not a dry eye at the cliffs. But we all knew there could have been no more beautiful ending for this magnificent man.

# THE TWO HIGHEST WOMEN IN THE WORLD

## A STORY

by Laura Waterman

Annie Smith Peck (1850–1935) and Fanny Bullock Workman (1859–1925) both made climbing history in the world's highest ranges during the first decade of the twentieth century. Annie Peck was a classics professor who turned full-time climber at age forty-six. The Andes were her field of action. She kept her expeditions small, lightweight, and low-budget, funded through lectures and articles about her adventures. The north peak of Huascarán in Peru is named for her. Fanny Bullock Workman and her husband, William Hunter Workman, explored, mapped, and climbed in the Karakoram and Himalaya. They possessed the wealth to hire guides, scientists, and hundreds of porters. At the time, Annie and Fanny were the two most prominent women in the world engaged in sustained high-altitude mountaineering. Laura was irresistibly drawn to writing a fictional account of their rivalry, told through the medium of Annie's letters to her brother.

▲ ▼ ▲

**Clarendon Hotel**
5th Ave., corner of 18th St.
New York City
Jan. 10, 1910

My dear brother,

I am sorry to learn in your recent letter that you took the bother to read those articles in the papers. I am finding it most irksome, this having to defend myself in the public press against Mrs. Workman's attack. All that I have written on the subject makes it plain that I claim nothing in the way of breaking records. If truth be told, I mainly blame my own inability. To boil water on the summit so as to take an accurate altitude reading with the hypsometer was, at the moment, beyond my powers. Believe me, George, I have been over and over this ground until I am weary of it. I had thought when I finally reached the summit of my magnificent Huascarán my troubles would be over. You can imaging how it vexes me that they rear in my face like Hercules's hundred-headed Hydra.

I have met the lady but once. She and Dr. Workman came to pay their respects after my return from Peru. I'd not been in New York a full week when they appeared here at my apartment in the Clarendon without prior announcement. I had them in, but my expedition gear—ice axes, crampons, the Mummery tent, eiderdown sleeping bag, camp stove and cook pots, even my woolen underwear—was in various stages of unpacking and airing out, draped over the furniture. I must admit, I felt rather caught out.

However, they did not stay long. I don't recall that we even sat down, but then, there was no place to sit! Well, I dare say such a scene was not unfamiliar to those two explorers. Have you seen their books? No expense spared. Mine, when it comes out, will look like humble pie. Their mountain photographs are compared with the great Sella's and given full-page treatment. Gilt-lettered bindings on a half-dozen titles about mapping the ice-wilds of the Karakoram. It was in the Nun Kun that Mrs. Workman set the altitude record for women, 23,300 feet.

They came, they said, to congratulate me on my Huascarán ascent, and for my part I was pleased to engage in a bit of mountaineer's talk. Their questions concerned the state of the crevasses and the angle of slope. Did the Mummery tent hold up well in strong winds? Did we use ropes clear to the summit? Did I have problems managing the native porters? Dr. Workman launched into a tale of how once in the Karakoram one hundred and fifty of their coolies had absconded in the dead of night with most of the supply of grain. It made me suppress a smile, since in our American Alpine Club circle the Workmans are notorious for their callous treatment of the natives.

As we chatted, Mrs. Workman's glance wandered over my gear. Her eyes are very large, and her eyebrows arched in a way that made clear she was reviewing the troops and they were found wanting. She is Governor Bullock's daughter, and I kept feeling myself reminded of that, though I have three times her education.

"I see you climb in knickerbockers, Miss Peck," she said. They were airing out across the back of the sofa.

"I've worn knickers ever since my Matterhorn climb in '95," I offered.

The eyebrows arched higher. "Well, you must find pants practical," she said.

"Indeed I do."

"A skirt, shortened to calf length, with puttees wrapped around the lower limbs, is an arrangement that has answered perfectly on all my expeditions," she countered.

"Don't you find a skirt hinders locomotion, Mrs. Workman?"

"Not in the least, Miss Peck."

Women say this, but it is obviously absurd. I flatter myself that at nearly sixty I can still slip on a pair of trousers with ease. I know it shocked our parents, but they found my degrees and professorships too intellectual, too distinguished, too *noticeable* for a lady. At least they didn't live to see notice turn to notoriety when I discovered audiences would pay a good deal more to hear me lecture on climbing mountains than they would pay to hear me drone on about ancient Greece.

But back to my point, George. I realize now this light talk was all subterfuge. What they really wanted to know was: What was Huascarán's altitude and how did I measure it? Dr. Workman asked me that. Mrs. W. had stepped away and appeared to be examining my ice ax. Her back was turned, but I was aware she held a little black notebook and was writing in it.

I tried to give Dr. Workman as full an answer as I could. They set great store in scientific measurements. Professor Fay of our Alpine Club has told me that their porters are turned into beasts of burden carrying the scientific gear alone, and that the Workmans themselves are positive bloodhounds when it comes to taking measurements of anything on the horizon, not to mention points up the glacier, passes, tent sites (they claim the world's highest), and, of course, summits. They have built a reputation for accuracy, though the club members are not above joking that the Workmans have a "measurement fixation." Be that as it may, I realized it was important to answer Dr. Workman as fully as I could.

After the ascent, I told him, I requested my two guides to estimate the height of the North Peak—that was the one we climbed—above the saddle, which we had measured with the hypsometer at 20,000 feet. I cautioned them to base their estimate on the angle of slope, the rate of ascent, and hours taken. Rudolf put it at 5000 feet; Gabriel, at 4200 feet. My own opinion, comparing this with my ascent of Orizaba, was 4000 feet. We had, I assured Dr. Workman, attempted to take measurements with the hypsometer at the summit, but the wind and cold had prevented us. So, this being an eye-estimate, I felt it important to err on the conservative side. Nonetheless, as it seemed to me certain Huascarán was above 23,800 feet, I informed Dr. Workman that if Huascarán's height is as much as 24,000 feet, which seems probable, I have the honor of breaking the *world's* record for men as well as women. As I finished speaking, George, the silence in the room thickened, and I had the queasy feeling that I had gone on too long.

Finally, Dr. Workman asked, "Miss Peck, am I right, then, in understanding you to say you made no instrumental measurements above the saddle?"

I replied in the affirmative, and at that moment Mrs. Workman pocketed her notebook and joined us. I thought her action odd, but stupidly assumed she had been noting the make of my ice ax. In the back of my mind was a story of how, in Spain, wearying of the conversation of their hostess, they both took out their notebooks and began writing up their observations of the day's travel.

As they were taking their leave—we were in the act of shaking hands on the threshold—Mrs. Workman, who had offered very little, said, "A pity about the hypsometer. That will cause no end of trouble."

And they were gone.

I thought all this so peculiar that I flew to my windows that front on the avenue to watch for when they emerged from the building. I fully intended to thrust out my head and shout, "Why did you even bother to come! Surely you must have read my article in *Harper's*." But something—the way Dr. Workman lowered his head to catch her words—stopped me. I watched them proceed along, side by side, not hurrying, as were all the other passersby. Yes, I thought, they fitted into the scene in the sense of not standing out, but it was as though a circle was inscribed around them. As a couple they formed an island. They moved uptown in step, her arm at rest in his, and I had the uncomfortable feeling that by thus observing them, I had opened the door on their private sitting room. I tell you, George, it made me turn away.

*You* read that article! I made perfectly clear my difficulty of measuring the altitude. Gabriel suggested halting a little below the summit for observations, and he was right. We both knew the wind would be far worse on top. As it was, even though we surrounded the hypsometer with the leather poncho in an attempt to break the wind, and struck match after match, we could not keep the candle burning. With Rudolf's help it might have been accomplished, but this faithless guide had his eye on the summit and had gone on ahead. You understand, one has to submerge the hypsometer in boiling water in order to obtain a correct reading of the altitude. It's a fussy, time-consuming operation more easily carried out in the laboratory at sea level than on a wind-scoured snow slope with fingers stiffening into claws and time on your heels. It was already past three, and we were not yet upon the highest point. At last Gabriel yelled in my ear: "It is useless." I knew that—the wind-driven snow was cutting the exposed flesh of my face like razors—but I wanted him to say it first. I tumbled the instruments into their sack—organization, I must confess, had gone by the boards. In fact, at the moment I believed it better to return alive, though ignorant of the exact height; but despite the discomfort to my person, my mind was torn with the terrible disappointment of not making the expected contribution to science. To think that I have probably broken the world's record and I am not able to prove it!

Please address your next letter to me here at the Clarendon, though before my reply, I will have moved several blocks south to where the rents better fit my budget.

As ever, yr. sister,
Annie Peck

Hotel Alabama
13-15 East 11th St.
Jan. 24, 1910

Dear George,

Your last letter asked me to keep you informed of the latest events in the "Workman affair," as you put it.

After their visit, I could not fathom how my failing to accurately measure Huascarán's height could make any real difference to them. To, in particular, her. Which shows you how little, at that moment, I understood Fanny Bullock Workman.

Because, George, it was only a few days later that an article appeared in the Philadelphia paper asserting that (and I quote): "Mrs. Workman, who claims to be the champion woman mountain scaler of the world, boldly challenged the claims of Miss Annie Peck to preeminence, and declared that the latter would have to submit proofs of her achievement or stand discredited."

This was followed by Mrs. Workman contracting the engineering firm in France with her instructions to triangulate Huascarán. An expensive step! No doubt she didn't want to take it until she had heard from me—the horse's mouth—the impossibility of ascertaining with certainty Huascarán's height. Knowing the Workmans' zeal for scientific accuracy, I suppose it should not vex me. But it does. I've read in the newspapers that the survey was to commence at sea level and work its way overland toward the Andes—and *my* peak. She has the right, I suppose. But I feel it a trespass. Generous of her to say in print that I was welcome to have *her* mountains measured. Even if I had half their fortune, I wouldn't spend it on engineers to go traipsing about the Himalaya checking up on her. It makes me laugh. Mostly it makes me ask myself: would she have troubled personally to fund a team of French surveyors to set off to Peru if I had been a man? No! Several men, including her own husband, have exceeded her altitude. This she accepts. Can it be that because we are of the same sex she is driven to this display of indignation?

Despite the fact that she is keeping her name (and mine) in the public press these days, I want to tell you that I have never heard the kind of criticism hurled at her that I seem to reap. It began after my victory on Huascarán. Because of *this* labor of hardship and love, I hear myself described as driven, relentless, ruthless, inspired by a lust for success, even egomaniacal. If I do appear this way, I see no fault in it. Though, Brother, I feel the sting. I don't hear such epithets thrown at other members of our American Alpine Club. They are men, and as such are permitted the single-mindedness that is necessary to achieve great ends. *She* escapes this name-calling. Why? Because she does her climbing with her husband. She *has* a husband. They make a team. They have wealth. This unbeatable combination ensures her protection, as it were, from her own behavior. No matter how "unwomanly."

I can write this way to you, George, since you among all our family have always encouraged my climbing.

Fondly, yr. sister,
Annie Peck

Feb. 2, 1910

Dear George,

Today I received a letter that I fear crushes my hopes. It is from Mrs. Workman. She plans to attend my talk at the Explorers Club next week, at which time she means to inform me of the results of her triangulation. I cannot assume that for me she has good news. Rather, it appears, she has appointed herself the bearer of my bad news.

By the way, George, I never mentioned what this little indulgence—the surveying of my peak—was costing them. *Thirteen thousand dollars.* You can well imagine how this makes my teeth ache: I who scrape up funding for my expeditions through the lecture circuit, by penning articles on my adventures, and by living in frayed hotels. Why, with half that sum I think I could break her record within the next six months in a way that there would be no question about.

However, my greater preoccupation, at the moment, is the fear that the club will not accept my altitude estimate. *Now* I rue that Gabriel and I did not try harder. If only I had been wearing Admiral Peary's Eskimo suit, which he had lent to me for the summit assault. But that lay in the bottom of a crevasse, lost in the act of lowering our gear down an ice wall. So on that dreadful summit day I had no wind-protecting layer, and my blood, I swear, was freezing. Perhaps my being a founding member of the club will count in my favor. But I am grasping at straws.

I take some consolation from a recent conversation with Professor Fay. He took pains to let me know he thought it disgraceful of Herschel Parker to launch a return expedition to Mount McKinley with the sole purpose being to discredit Mr. Cook. Professor Fay said a man's word should be believed. But there goes Parker, Cook's photographs in hand, to prove Cook never did reach the summit of the North American continent! Professor Fay has told me the club has chosen not to back Parker in his pursuit of disproving Cook. I draw some little comfort from that. At least no one is calling into question whether I *climbed* my mountain.

I was invited to give my Huascarán lecture at our Alpine Club, but since that august body is in the process of passing judgment on my altitude estimate, I have declined. My dignity demanded that. Since the Explorers Club has no quarrel with me, I have accepted their invitation. *This,* dear brother, will be the arena of my second meeting with Mrs. Fanny Bullock Workman.

Think of me.

With affection,<br>Annie Peck

Feb. 11, 10:00 A.M.

Dear George,

Achilles (Mrs. W.) has fought Hector (me) and Troy (my record) has fallen. At least that is how it would at first appear. But read on!

I don't know if you have been in the Explorers Club. The hall is grand, darkly paneled with arched windows, the walls studded with horns and heads and hooves, magnificent trophies that gaze down with glass eyes on those strutting about in furs and glitter. Mrs. Workman flourished a sable boa. As you know, I would rather stand alone at the verge of a precipice than mingle with society, but I can report I managed to feel up to snuff in Mother's pearl choker. Though Mrs. W. displayed diamonds, I calculated the score a draw, since I was the evening's speaker.

I had no sooner entered the hall when Mrs. Workman stationed herself before me, straight-backed as a general. She isn't very tall, George, but she piles up her hair and wears hats that give her the appearance of height. "Miss Peck," she announced in that clipped British tone she acquired from living most of her life abroad, "you have not the honor of breaking the world's record for men or women. My two highest ascents, 22,568 and 23,300 feet, debar you from that honor in the case of women. As for men, a number have made ascents higher than yours, in particular, my husband, Dr. William Hunter Workman."

At this notice, Dr. Workman, who had been standing at her side, executed the slightest of bows. With his straight nose and head of thick white hair, I must say he made a dignified appearance in evening clothes.

She went on to proclaim that my Huascarán was not the world's highest mountain, or even the loftiest in this hemisphere. The North Peak topped out at 21,812 feet. The South Peak was measured at 22,187 feet, if I am to believe her extravagantly expensive survey. "So, Miss Peck," she concluded, "you must be satisfied with having ascended the highest mountain climbed by an American in the western hemisphere." At that moment, Dr. Workman slipped his hand under his wife's elbow and they excused themselves before I had said a word, wheeling off in tandem.

Thinking about it, I have the conviction that this whole scene had been arranged. Her role was to fire the broadside, and his to preclude retaliation. Perhaps they thought they were doing me a kindness. After all, what would my rejoinder have been? To throw my glove at her feet and so call her out?

A pity she has set herself up as my rival. We have so much in common. For instance, we have both discovered that the road to freedom for women is not to maintain a residence, not to be "at home on Thursdays," not to be forever "presenting compliments" and "expressing regrets." We must feel similarly that the pride women take in their place behind the tea urn is a trap. It appears to me that Mrs. W. is as captivated—as held in thrall—by mountains as I am. Perhaps, too, when she has returned to the confining spaces of indoor living, she finds herself stumbling over her ice ax still propped behind the chair, and cannot pack away her tent and eiderdown, though it has been airing out for weeks. If this is her predicament as well, I would risk saying that we are sisters under the skin.

Then, I would like to ask her if she feels her achievements have been taken seriously. I cannot say that I do. Some of the club members, namely Professor Fay, are kind to me. But there is a ring of condescension I cannot overlook. On the title page of the Workmans' *Ice-Bound Heights of the Mustagh,* I count twelve memberships and honors in mountaineering organizations listed below her name, as if this constituted proof of her acceptance. But does she really feel accepted in this man's world?

Bear with me, George, I am coming to the odd part of the evening.

Aside from her husband, her entourage included a young lady, her daughter, who I understand was brought up in England. Their school system permits the packing off of very young children to be housed, fed, and educated with no trouble to the parents, save expense. This, no doubt, was a convenience to the Workmans, who live out of their trunks and have no more permanent address than I.

As I began my lecture—they had taken seats near the front—Mrs. Workman leaned forward, peering up, then down, her row. Then she proceeded to remove her left-hand glove, which extended to the elbow. Another darting look, and the left glove was back on and the right one worked off. From the podium I made a quick survey of how the ladies chose to deploy their gloves, but discerned no clear consensus. She went on like this, twitching off one, then the other, all accompanied, as you might imagine, with a certain degree of rustle, like a furtive mouse in a back room. Others began to notice. There was a nudging of one's neighbor, turning of heads, even whispering. *My* words, I was beginning to think, were falling on inattentive ears. Finally, her husband put his hand over hers, and as I watched she raised her face to him, and those dark arched eyebrows that give her such a commanding aspect—Caesar at the van—appeared as if stuck on for a play. Not long after that, they stood and edged out of the row, causing people to draw aside their knees. They walked down the long aisle, his hand gripping her arm above the elbow, the daughter in their wake. Eyes followed them out of the hall, and once again I knew I was in danger of losing my audience.

Naturally, I feared because of this disturbance that my talk had come off poorly. Was *this* triumph to be undermined by *her* as well? But afterward I was besieged by questions and congratulations. I'll give you a sample from a gentleman I recognized as one of Professor Fay's companions on his ascents in the Canadian Rockies:

"Well, Miss Peck, splendid work," he boomed. "Was it 1905? You said your first attempt was back in 1905?"

"In 1904," I replied.

"Ah, yes. And seven attempts, was it?"

"Only six. I never like to give up what I have undertaken."

"Ha! Ha! Admirable. Whymper on the Matterhorn. Seven for him. The big ones must be wooed, eh, Miss Peck? Think of it! A mite of a thing like you. I offer my hearty congratulations. Indeed I do!" He pumped my hand and lumbered off.

More than once, as I was being thus congratulated by similar mustached and bearded gentlemen, I opened my mouth to say: You understand, sir, my only real pleasure is the satisfaction of going where no man has been before and few can follow. But always, at that moment, the gentleman would drop my hand and turn into the crowd.

For me the evening was over. I could not dislodge Mrs. Workman's behavior with the gloves from my mind. I was about to ascend to the dais and retrieve my papers when I felt a tap on my arm, turned, and faced—the daughter. Immediately I noticed her eyebrows resembled the mother's. She had been sent back, she informed me, by her parents with the task of expressing regrets at their early departure, though she made no *explanation*. Perhaps the daughter saw my displeasure in my face. I'm sure I took no pains to disguise it. I simply nodded in acknowledgment that I had heard. I meant, then, to turn away, since I could see that others wanted to speak with me. My dress shoes were pinching my feet, and all I desired was to end the evening and return to my rooms. But there was something in the daughter's face that held me. "Miss Peck," she said, "You did it yourself. You did everything—yourself."

At that moment, Professor Fay pushed between us. He had with him another gentleman, a Professor Hiram Bingham, who, Fay told me, was planning an expedition to Peru for a year hence. Professor Bingham wrung my hand, and, removing his cigar, extended to me his sincerest congratulations. He then informed me that his goal, the Coropuna massif, might exceed Aconcagua in height. "Fay has given me to understand you're an expert on travel in the mountains of Peru," he said, proceeding, then, to barrage me with questions. But I can assure you, George, he got very little out of me, though he made the air blue with his cigar smoke. Besides, others were thrusting forth their hands, though their congratulations continued in much the same vein and I can remember little of it now. It wasn't until I had re-gained the quiet of my rooms that I recalled my welling feelings of triumph over the daughter's words.

Yr. fond sister,
Annie Peck

P.S.: This morning I realized the full implication of what Professor Bingham told me. Coropuna higher than Aconcagua? If that is the case, I can assure you, Brother, it is I who intend to be first on the ground. I shall set my mind immediately to the task of raising the necessary funds. This massif has five summits, I learned last night. Think of it! One of them might be *the world's highest*.

# THE RISE AND FALL OF A SHORT-RUN DEITY

O n Labor Day weekend in 1968, the circle of climbers we climbed with in the New York area held a joint excursion with a group from Boston at the East's highest cliff, on Cannon Mountain in New Hampshire's Franconia Notch. Guy and another New York leader were matched with two seconds from Boston to climb the classic Whitney-Gilman Ridge. One of the seconds was a silent but observant sixteen-year-old who had not a bit of difficulty whatsoever with the hardest moves. When we next met him, two years later, it was at Connecticut's Ragged Mountain cliff, where he was pioneering the hardest routes yet done in the state. After that the pace quickened. Within the next two to four years Henry Barber was generally acknowledged as the greatest pure rock climber in the world. It was inordinately flattering to us that he always recalled our early acquaintance with a show of pleasure and affection. Of course he had to be a major figure in our history of Northeastern climbing, for which we wrote most of the following account of his meteoric rise and fall. We have added some personal recollections to this retelling. Henry Barber is also a major player in the (on the whole) cheerier "Anniversary Waltz in Pinnacle Gully," which follows.

**Source:** Adapted from Chapter 18, "Streibert and Barber, " and other passages in *Yankee Rock & Ice.*

▲ ▼ ▲

**A sportswriter once said of a flamboyant and controversial owner of the Washington** Redskins, "George Preston Marshall slipped into town last night at the head of a seventy-six-piece brass band." In much this spirit, Henry Barber stole onto the center stage of the rock-climbing world. Wherever "Hot Henry" went, climbers knew it.

Henry Barber was a lanky, awkward, rawboned, brash, and headstrong teenager whose relentless energy failed to find adequate outlets in baseball or schoolboy fistfights. At age sixteen he finally found an arena equal to his Herculean energies: rock climbing. He began climbing with the Boston chapter of the Appalachian Mountain Club, then regarded as a conservative bastion of old values and low climbing standards, where rapid progress to difficult climbing was frowned on. While other top-grade climbers of his time enjoyed disparaging the AMC, Henry never did, remembering his start there as "the best thing that ever happened to me." Rapidly going through early mentors such as D. Byers and George Meyers (before the latter moved to Yosemite), he soon branched out on his own with a string of younger partners—Oriel Sole Costa, Rick Hatch, Ajax Greene, Steve Hendricks, Chip Lee.

Barber had everything going for him. To begin with, he had a natural aptitude for climbing: "the single most talented climber I've ever seen," his great predecessor, Jim McCarthy, called him. His most visible trait was his phenomenal energy. Where other young hotshots might preen at the local bar after climbing a new route at the top of the standard, Henry would exhaust his seconds by climbing three or four such routes in a day—then hit the bars most of the night and be up at dawn to climb the next day.

Almost alone of the 1970s star climbers (Rich Romano was another exception) Barber did not follow a regimen of exercise and specialized training. Instead (like Romano) he simply climbed all the time: he trained to climb by climbing. In his early days Barber had converted his family's basement into a training gymnasium, doing chin-ups on paint stirrers nailed to the wall and building a "Foops machine" on which to practice the moves he'd need for the historic second ascent of the then-hardest climb in the Northeast, *Foops*. But after 1971 he ignored training and simply climbed full time. In 1971 he climbed 260 days of the year; in 1972, 350; in 1973, 350. His response to competition was electric. He loved the limelight.

Barber's biggest weapon, however, was neither his talent nor his energy. It was his confidence. The venerated British alpinist Geoffrey Winthrop Young had identified the three requirements for achieving the highest standards of difficulty in rock climbing as "physique, confidence, and endurance." If Colorado's Layton Kor or, in the East, Rich Goldstone had demonstrated the advantages of a splendid physique, and if California's Warren Harding or the East's John Stannard had shown what inexhaustible reserves of endurance could do, Henry Barber now arrived to show what power lay in unlimited, unquenchable, all-ruling confidence.

"An instant's failure of will or confidence," Young had warned, "will disturb the delicate adjustments of balance as fatally as a broken leg." Barber uniquely possessed that unshakable will and confidence. He firmly believed, when approaching a previously unclimbed problem, that he was the man who could do it. In the most precarious situations, rising beneath a seemingly insurmountable roof or blank face, his last protection receding far below him, he never wavered in the quiet belief that he would find a way up.

As Carlyle said of Robespierre, "Doubt dwelt not in him."

In 1972, his apprenticeship completed, Barber pulled off the first of what became his trademark: a concentrated blitz of a single climbing area, during which he left all onlookers breathless and drastically altered the local standard. In 1972 it was New Hampshire's Cathedral Ledge. In a whirlwind of free climbing, mostly with Bob Anderson as partner, Barber put up eleven new routes that year, nine of them at a level of 5.9 or better, including the cliff's first 5.11, *Lichen Delight*. The upper left section of the cliff was so thoroughly saturated with his new routes that it became known as the "Barber Shop." Many of these lines were old aid routes nailed by others. Barber's demonstration of what could be climbed free gave the first impetus to a movement away from aid in the north country, although New Hampshire climbers never did renounce aid as devoutly as did their counterparts at the Shawangunks.

Wherever Barber went, he created new standards. At Whitehorse, he put in the first 5.10, *Beelzebub*. At Cannon, he put in the first 5.10, *Whaleback Crack*. Down at Crow Hill, he put in the first 5.11 in Massachusetts, *Jane*. At Ragged, he put in what was seen at the time as Connecticut's first 5.10, *Subline,* although subsequent second thoughts upgraded the Streibert-Merritt masterpiece, *Aid Crack,* from 5.9 to 5.10, upstaging Barber this once. All of these "firsts" were done in 1972, and all with Bob Anderson as his partner. Obviously Anderson was climbing very well too, a fact often overlooked—it was a quality of Barber that he put everyone around him in the shade.

One of Henry's most important contributions to the changing character of the sport was the transformation of the nature and purpose of Boston-area practice climbing. Hitherto, Boston climbers had congregated on weekday evenings or nontraveling weekends at Quincy Quarries, Black and White Rocks, and other crags where they climbed in miniature the same kinds of climbs, and at approximately the same levels of difficulty, to which they were accustomed when they went to the Gunks or the north country. Barber led a movement toward bouldering on several man-made stone walls—a thirteen- to seventeen-foot-high overpass near Kenmore Square on which more than thirty distinct routes were developed in the early 1970s; a similar construction in Olmstead Park; the Waban Arches, supporting a viaduct for the Chestnut Hill Reservoir; Echo Bridge, another part of that viaduct; and Charlesgate, a retaining wall for an overpass leading to one of the bridges over the Charles River. These were lower than Quincy or Black and White, and (to say the least) not aesthetically situated. But the level of difficulty was miles harder. At Kenmore Square, with few exceptions, routes started at 5.9 and included at least three at 5.11. Barber's message was that the path to higher standards elsewhere lay in diligently practicing the most difficult moves imaginable at home, regardless of aesthetic considerations. After 1971, ambitious Boston-area climbers logged more hours at Kenmore Square and the Waban Arches than at Quincy or Black and White (though less zealous climbers understandably preferred the old haunts). Barber had more to do with this change than any other individual.

After 1972 Barber widened his theater of operations until it took in the whole planet, as he systematically descended upon Yosemite Valley, England's crags, Australia, Africa, the Soviet Union, and various other spots, significantly altering standards wherever he went. An aura of competitive superiority—a "fastest gun in the West" syndrome—grew up about him. He

became the first major American "rock star," featured on nationwide tele-
vision specials and a familiar face in climbing magazines and posters. Young
climbers of the mid-1970s had to climb in white painter's pants because
that's what Hot Henry wore. He became the first Northeastern climber to
make a living as a climber, combining lecture fees and endorsements with
serving as a representative for climbing outfitters.

Perhaps even more significant was his influence on climbing ethics and
style. Following the lead of John Stannard and Steve Wunsch, he became
an uncompromising proponent of free climbing, disdaining any form of aid.
As the region's most prominent superclimber, he powerfully pulled an entire generation of climbers in the direction of high standards of ethics and
style.

For a few years after he became a world-renowned star, Barber continued to climb frequently in the Northeast. He never forgot his home base and
the beloved cliffs where he got his start.

At the Shawangunks in 1972, he had made a lightning raid to pull off the
coveted second ascent of the giant roof on *Foops,* the East's first serious
5.11, first climbed by John Stannard in 1967. It had taken almost five years
since Stannard's first ascent, an unusually long time for such a celebrated
plum to ripen, and a tribute to how far ahead of his time Stannard had been.
Barber's success on *Foops* in effect raised the curtain on a new epic period
at the Gunks, 1972 through 1974.

Near the end of 1972 a new guidebook to the Shawangunks appeared. In
it were still listed some thirty-three aid routes. Aware that aid climbing had
traditionally involved copious placement and removal of rock-damaging pi-
tons, Stannard and Barber regarded this publicizing of so much aid as a direct threat to the success of the burgeoning "clean climbing" movement, not
to mention a challenge to their free-climbing skills.

Speedily, with the happy compliance of Steve Wunsch and John Bragg,
Barber and Stannard began a systematic campaign to eradicate aid from the
Shawangunk scene. In 1973 all but five of the thirty-three were freed. Some
turned out to go free at a relatively moderate level (5.9 then being moderate in this league), but more than half proved to be 5.11 or harder. Some of
these tasked the finest efforts of the front four. At least half a dozen were
significantly harder than *Foops.* Stannard was almost invariably involved
in these, but Barber (despite being active at half a dozen other climbing

areas that year) was in on eleven, including some of the toughest.

Throughout the mid-1970s Barber was a presence in the New Hampshire climbing scene, residing (when not globetrotting) in the nearby town of Conway. In 1977 he took an interest in a cliff in the Adirondacks and, in a single season, in the words of a local guidebook editor, "brought our freeclimbing here near the level of New Hampshire's."

We recall one day during those golden years of splendor on the rocks, when we were talking with a bunch of local climbers on an uncrowded weekday morning at the back of New Hampshire's premier climbing equipment shop. Several of those in the store that morning were among New Hampshire's best climbers, but no one made a particular fuss, because they lived there. But then the front door opened and Hot Henry walked in. All activity and conversation ceased, all eyes turned, almost as if everyone held their breath. Henry passed down the aisles with a smile for everyone, a friendly word to an old climbing buddy, a thrilling nod to a young woman behind the counter; he had a radiance comparable to Jack Kennedy campaigning through a crowd of primary voters, or the Beatles moving through a phalanx of fans, or Babe Ruth with a bunch of knothole kids. No special event, just Henry Barber coming into town for some shopping. This inconsequential incident remains in our minds as a vivid demonstration of the extraordinary aura surrounding the world's hottest rock star.

This celebrity's public career received a severe jolt from an incident on Africa's Mount Kilimanjaro. His climbing partner, Rob Taylor, was badly injured, rescued through a supreme effort on his own and Henry's part, but then left to be evacuated and to recuperate in a primitive African hospital without as much attention and solace from Barber as he felt was due. Embittered, Taylor wrote magazine articles and a fictionalized book about the incident, painting Barber in a most unflattering light.

Was Barber blameworthy for what happened on that remote ice cliff in Africa? For years it's been said that your take on this incident depended on whether you were a friend of Henry or a friend of Rob. It might also depend on your politics: whether you are someone who instinctively dislikes the top dog or someone who automatically accords respect to number one.

We like to recount one anecdote as having some vague relevance to whether Henry acted responsibly on Kilimanjaro or not. One day at the Shawangunks, we noticed a sizable crush of spectators crowded around the base of a cliff where one figure was executing a succession of incredibly difficult bouldering moves. (This was before Kilimanjaro.) The figure, of course, turned out to be Hot Henry: who else would attract such a crowd? Laura was off on a climb somewhere, Guy was sans partner. So he went through the crowd to say hello to Henry and ask him if he'd like to do a climb. Darn right, said Henry, all these clowns stand around and watch me boulder and nobody asks if I'd like to do a climb! Noticing Guy had a rope and gear, he didn't stop to fetch any of his own stuff, but led the way to a less frequented part of the cliffs, the base of a route appropriately called *Farewell to Arms*. There Guy observed several things. First, Henry never asked who would lead; he assumed he would. Second, he plucked just two pieces of protection from Guy's rack.

Since Guy knew the first pitch involved two long traverses, he thought, "Oh boy, I'm not going to be very protected. If I come off, it'll be a long swing." But he was wrong: Henry ignored the need for any protection for himself, doing the hardest moves without nearby "pro," but he placed the two pieces precisely where they would protect Guy on the traverses. To Guy this signified (a) Henry was so familiar with this climb that he knew exactly which two pieces could be used at these two points, and (b)—the point that bears on the Kilimanjaro affair—he was looking out for his partner's interests, not his own.

In a moment of relaxation at his house one evening—this was after Kilimanjaro—Henry talked about the incident. His resentment of Taylor and his well-publicized writings was undisguised. He pointed out that in Africa they had been warned of two things: (a) never go into the jungle at night, and (b) never go into the jungle alone. After securing the injured Taylor at a high bivouac and descending to the edge of vegetation, Henry had to go for help several miles through the jungle—(a) at night, and (b) alone. He had pushed himself through the night, despite being exhausted from the superhuman effort of climbing and then getting his partner down to where he could be safely secured on the bivouac ledge. He had set the rescue in motion in the fastest possible time. After more than twenty-four hours of all-out effort, he did not return with the rescuers.

As for whether he should have stayed around to comfort his partner through his long recuperation in that miserable primitive hospital, Henry candidly told us it's just not in him. He's not a warm, sentimental, comforting person; that's not his nature. Yes, he can be faulted for that, but there was no way he could have played that role. For a partner who wanted that kind of attention and concern, Henry fell short.

Not everyone might share Taylor's need for that kind of comfort and fuss. On that evening at Henry's house, one of us had just received word of a personal tragedy few have to deal with—but Henry's reticence on the matter was welcome in our case. No sentimental fuss was wanted. People differ on their reactions and needs in these matters.

Back to Henry's life. Kilimanjaro changed everything. The whole affair, and Taylor's writing about it, had a traumatic impact on Hot Henry's place in the climbing scene. In a short space of time, Barber went from being the darling of the climbing world to an object of scorn in the eyes of many critics. With his brassy candor and undisguised egotism, Barber had been respected and imitated but never loved. Critics were quick to jump on the fallen idol. Within a year or two, this young-man-in-a-hurry who had welcomed the limelight retreated from the public stage almost completely. Though he continued to climb, he avoided publicity, never reported first ascents, and deliberately drew back from the competition at the cutting edge of the sport.

It had been a glorious five years or so. Barber compares with but a half dozen figures in the entire short history of Northeastern rock climbing—some of whom the reader has met in earlier stories: Underhill, Wiessner, and Kraus, plus certainly Jim McCarthy and John Stannard and possibly Sam Streibert. Of those, only Wiessner climbed as widely throughout the region. In terms of impact on the sport, Wiessner was too far ahead of American standards to elicit emulation. But Barber was always just one step ahead of a crowd of hot young climbers in each area. He drew them after him like hounds to a fox. His impact on climbing standards was therefore probably greater than anyone's.

One of his contemporaries went so far as to say that Barber had "a greater influence than any [other] climber who ever lived," obviously a judgment difficult to defend, but based on the observation that Barber came along at a time when standards were ready to rise—so when he showed the way, everyone leaped after him. Once everyone caught up to his level, further progress inevitably slowed, making Henry possibly "the last great name in North American rock climbing," to quote another contemporary judgment.

That statement is also difficult to defend, but it is based on the theory that further advances will inevitably occur so slowly, or at least so spasmodically, that no one will ever again stand out ahead of the pack or raise an entire region's sights as dramatically as did Hot Henry Barber in his days of wine and roses.

# ANNIVER-SARY WALTZ IN PINNACLE GULLY

## FOUR CLIMBING GENERATIONS ON HUNTINGTON RAVINE'S CLASSIC ROUTE

**W**e first met Julian Whittlesey as an interviewee for our work on Northeastern climbing history. By this time he was restlessly exploring his upper eighties, but, as indicated in the story that follows, we found him (and his wife) fabulously inquisitive, opinionated, articulate, and tirelessly roving over a diverse encyclopedia of interests. After our initial interview, we returned, mainly just to enjoy another sparkling evening in their company—with the results that Guy recorded in the following story.

**Source:** Published first in the December 1990 issue of *Appalachia,* and again in *Yankee Rock & Ice.*

▲ ▼ ▲

**"The Fall of the Maiden's Tears"** was what the early White Mountains romantics called it. Sometimes it was known as Huntington's Cascades, after Joshua Huntington, the first weather observer to winter over on Mount Washington's hostile summit. Even earlier the botanist William Oakes styled its locale "the dark ravine," to contrast it with Tuckerman's airy, friendly, sun-drenched spaciousness. A 1924 visitor, cringing under "the majestic headwall," muttered, "Instead of beckoning to us as did the Tuckerman Headwall, it seemed to tell us to go back."

Today we call it Pinnacle Gully. It is the hidden treasure of Huntington's, that "dark ravine" on New Hampshire's Mount Washington, with its bristling crags, narrow ice-choked couloirs, and greenish-black jutting precipices. In the middle of Huntington Ravine's headwall, a huge rock monolith occupies the center ground: the Pinnacle. Behind the north side of the buttress—the side that never sees the sun, of course—a delicate mist floats softly down a rotten gully of lush green moss set amongst crumbling rock.

In winter, if you peer behind this buttress, you find that the snow fan steepens sharply, ending in a near-vertical wall of blue-green ice swooping up, right against the imposing north wall of the Pinnacle. Above snakes a narrow, steep, dark, evil band of ice, overhung by jutting green-black crags. At least half the time the whole is suffused with a noisy cacophony of raging wind, blowing ice particles, hissing spindrift, ominous foreboding. On rare good days, though, the majestic setting is inspiring, a privileged place where one can walk among the mountain gods.

### The First Ascent

The earliest ice climbers were daunted: visiting Everest veteran Noel Odell of Great Britain climbed the ice on the south flank of the Pinnacle, but left this north side alone. America's best 1920s climber, Harvard philosophy professor Robert Underhill, hailed Pinnacle Gully as "incomparably the most difficult and dangerous" route on the mountain. He climbed the first pitch but then backed off, intimidated. An eager young generation of Harvard alpinists, led by Brad Washburn, Ad Carter, Charlie Houston, and Bob Bates, nursed ambitions to make the first ascent.

Before these valiant sons of Harvard could manage to do so, a pair of inexperienced students from a small college in New Haven known locally as Yale ("Goodnight, Poor Harvard") University, pulled off the coup of the decade by climbing Pinnacle Gully. In 1930 Julian Whittlesey was a remarkable young man, as attested by his brilliantly varied subsequent career as a New

Deal planner, designer of such cities as Reston, Virginia, and Kitimat, British Columbia. He also designed slum clearance projects in Asia and Africa, and pioneered innovative archaeological techniques in the Mediterranean.

As a young architecture student, he and classmate Sam Scoville had been involved in a couple of unsuccessful attempts on Pinnacle Gully under the leadership of Yale's best ice climber of that day, William Willcox. Convinced that a two-person team would be faster and therefore safer, Whittlesey and Scoville arrived in Pinkham Notch in a top-down Buick, heedless of below-zero temperatures and "wildly blowing snow." On February 8, 1930, they plodded up to the ravine, carrying a huge canvas rucksack and long wooden ice axes. In an amazing, sustained all-day effort in horrendous conditions, Whittlesey and Scoville chopped steps up pitch after pitch of the ice in Pinnacle Gully. Dismissing the magnitude of their feat, Whittlesey later commented, "The trip back at twenty below in an open top-down car overnight to New Haven on roads that others could not deal with—hence no traffic—was perhaps more notable."

### Changing Worlds and Ice Axes

That top-down car existed a long seventy years ago, in a different America. Herbert Hoover and Prohibition ruled the land. In February 1930, the sheet music to "Stardust" had just been published. Big Bill Tilden dominated tennis, while Sonja Henie won her fourth consecutive world figure-skating title. New York Yankee management received, "with dignity, scorn, and a deal of silence," Babe Ruth's absurd demand for $85,000 a year, a salary higher than President Hoover's ("I had a better year than Hoover," explained the Babe). A Fifth Avenue shop sold men's suits for $26.50. On Broadway, Wanamaker's offered "Sprightly Spring Frocks" for $9.75, ladies' oxfords, slippers, and high-heel shoes at $2.95 a pair, and men's shirts at $1.95. Studebaker's latest "long and low-slung chassis," with a seventy-horsepower engine and genuine mohair upholstery, commanded a price of $895. Loew's Theatre offered an "all-talking" film version of *The Virginian* starring Gary Cooper, and Charles Lindbergh suggested a radical innovation in aeroplanes: "a shield designed to make both cockpits windproof." The House Judiciary Committee formally sat to hear "The Star-Spangled Banner," sung by Mrs. Elsie Jorss-Reilley of Washington, D.C., and Mrs. Grace Evelyn Boudlair of Baltimore and played by the Navy Band, with a view to deciding whether to make the song the national anthem. The ladies wished "to refute the argument that it is pitched too high for popular singing." One witness expressed concern that "the tune is suspiciously like an Old English drinking song."

The world has changed much since Hoover and Lindbergh and Whittlesey and Scoville. Well, actually, the world of ice climbing changed little for the first forty of those sixty years. For four decades Pinnacle Gully remained as Underhill had classified it: "incomparably the most difficult and dangerous" ice route in New England. It was the Grand Prix, the Wimbledon center court, the Super Bowl of winter climbing.

Beginning in 1969, a revolution in ice tools and techniques made much more difficult climbing possible. Ice axes with sharply drooped picks, serrated teeth, and much shorter handles, plus new kinds of crampons and ice screws, gave climbers security for hanging on ice of extreme verticality. Suddenly new routes boasting undreamed-of difficulty absorbed the attention of a new generation of New Hampshire climbers. All gullies in Huntington Ravine now seemed easy, and Pinnacle Gully was routinely soloed by the young tigers.

But from a purely aesthetic standpoint, Huntington is still a magnificent setting, and Pinnacle Gully is still its hidden jewel. Among the truly classic lines of New England ice, most discerning climbers, of whatever generation, still rank that twisting band of blue-green ice overhung with green-black crags as one of the three or four finest natural lines in the East. One of the best of the modern ice hard men has said, "Although I have been up that gully over one hundred times, my stomach always takes a flop when I see the cold green ice bulging out on the left side, guarded by the overhanging rock that looms overhead. To be there in 1930 with alpenstocks, hemp rope, ten-point crampons, and looking up at ice that is far steeper than anything the climber had previously contemplated, is an awesome concept."

## Whittlesey Revisited

Sixty years to the day after the first ascent of Pinnacle Gully, this author enjoyed an interesting and different sort of experience in this singular place.

In the fall of 1989, my wife, climbing partner, and coauthor, Laura, and I made a lunchtime pilgrimage to the Connecticut home of Julian Whittlesey. At age eighty-four he is still a dazzlingly innovative mind, and his wife, the beautiful and beloved Eunice, a former Broadway actress and his colleague in archaeological research, is equally remarkable. In their hilltop backyard Whittlesey had built a slender tower of vertical pipes soaring 107 feet into the clear autumnal sky. A few short and narrow pipes were stuck in horizontally at intervals, and these, Whittlesey alleged, constituted a ladder. The purpose was to suspend a pendulum so that he could study something esoteric about the Earth's movement. (Still many fascinating things to find out when you're only eighty-four.)

That day his pendulum had, to use nonscientific terminology, got stuck. So he ordered his visiting climbers to scamper up and fix it. The tower of pipes looked frail, but he assured us that his friend Bucky (Buckminster Fuller) had designed it to be perfectly stable. Accordingly, with considerable apprehension, we dug out our climbing gear and Laura led all the way to the 107-foot top, placing protection around the pipes en route. An impressive lead, I thought, but the 1930 conqueror of Pinnacle Gully took it as a routine procedure for climbers or those interested in studying the movement of pendulums and planets.

Back on the ground, after a few hours, filled with absolutely scintillating discourse from the Whittleseys on a broad range of subjects, we reluctantly prepared to leave. Julian ducked into the house a moment and emerged with a capacious heavy canvas Zenith rucksack with leather straps and buckles still intact, proclaimed it the pack that had climbed Pinnacle Gully in 1930, and, disclaiming any intention of further mountaineering ventures (being too busy exploring other frontiers), thrust it upon us to keep.

In the exhilaration of the moment, conscious that next winter would mark exactly sixty years since his historic first ascent, I promised Julian Whittlesey that his 1930 Zenith pack would go up to Pinnacle Gully again, on February 8, 1990.

### A Partner
### for the Waltz

As winter approached, I eyed that canvas monstrosity and wondered if I could maintain the balance modern ice climbing technique requires with that thing loaded and sagging far down my back. Laura, more sensible, disclosed she had little zest for a full day's drive and plod up the ravine for such a duty. The project and promise teetered.

Then, at a gathering of climbing friends where I recounted the tale of visiting Whittlesey, Henry Barber demanded to know if I had a partner for the anniversary climb. Back in the 1970s, the youthful "Hot Henry" had set the world afire with his brilliant climbing on both rock and ice. Unlike many modern stars, Henry always remembered from whence he came, and deeply respected the achievements of those pioneers in the realm of verticality on whose shoulders his generation stood to accomplish their great advances. He wished to join in honoring the anniversary of Pinnacle Gully's first ascent.

At first we spoke bravely of doing it in the old style: straight-angled ice axes, ten-point crampons, chopping steps all the way. Our courage failed us. We wanted the security of Chouinard-era drooped axes, front points, and ice screws that anchored securely. So we decided that the 1930 Zenith pack would constitute tribute enough.

To add a little flavor, I decided to don a 1930s-style straw hat for the occasion. Henry suggested the notorious Mount Washington wind would surely blow it far out across the state, but I pointed out that if I was wearing it, it would be affixed to a sharp-pointed object and thus would be stable.

On the morning of the climb, Henry made sure the contrast in our two generations was as distinct as that between mine and Julian Whittlesey's. I wore my usual old-style, unfashionable wool Air Force pants, plain tubular gaiters, and L. L. Bean parka, all in drab blues and grays. Henry is a Patagonia sales rep. So he emerged for the day in flashy scarlet windpants, neon green sweater, and other brightly colored accoutrements of the latest climbing fashion. With my canvas Zenith pack and straw skimmer to suggest the 1930s generation, we had all bases well covered.

We made an odd couple. I'm of the second, or post-Whittlesey, generation of climbers, while Henry is in the vanguard of the next climbing generation, with John Bragg, John Bouchard, and Rick Wilcox. Physically, he's big, I'm little. He has a mustache and no beard, I a beard and no mustache. Comparing our relative climbing abilities, grace, and professional reputations, Henry and I rank respectively as William Shakespeare and the writer who composed the obscure "Directions for Assembling Your Jiffy Lawn Chair" and other dramatic farces. During the salad days of his climbing youth, a globetrotting Henry visited fifty-three countries and formed lasting friendships from East Germany to Australia. In almost six decades on this planet, I've visited Canada twice briefly, but otherwise the only foreign countries

I've been in are Florida and California (once each, more than a quarter century ago). An occasional expedition to the Adirondacks constitutes my western trip for the year. Like Thoreau, I travel far in East Corinth.

### The Sixtieth-Anniversary Climb

At the Harvard Mountaineering Club cabin in the floor of the ravine, Henry and I were joined by the two young caretakers who capably patrol Huntington and Tuckerman Ravines in winter. They kindly broke trail through the new snow as the older and yet older generations moved up the slope toward our quest to honor the oldest generation and its historic climb of sixty years before. The weather was splendid, and, in midweek, we had the magnificent "dark ravine" all to ourselves—we thought.

We paused to put on crampons, sort gear, and take photographs at a rock outcrop about two hundred feet below and a like distance to one side of the base of our route. From here the incomparable prospect of Pinnacle ice gleamed above us. We saw, far below, another party of two emerge from the woods and follow our footsteps up the fan. Soon it became clear that the leader was (a) moving rapidly, and (b) heading not toward us for a friendly word, but straight toward the base of Pinnacle Gully. Evidently this party wished to move ahead of us on the route.

To Henry's and my generation this was a lamentable breach of etiquette. With my straw skimmer serving as hard hat, I had no wish to have another party showering ice from above. As for Henry, his old competitive instincts as the "fastest gun in the West," when he outperformed all other climbers wherever he went, took over: Hot Henry never turned down a challenge.

Having my crampons already on, I grabbed our rope and headed for the base of the ice. I got there first and began quickly throwing out rope at the most advantageous belay stance. The young leader of the challenging party arrived next and took up his own stance at the other corner of the ice. My automatic instinct in the mountains, to a fault, is to engage others I meet in friendly greeting. Many a party or individual seeking quiet solitude in the peaceful hills has been driven batty by my insistence on animated conversation. But on this occasion all attempts at good cheer and repartee met heavy sailing: the other party was not in a friendly mood. Clearly they had sized up the age of the party next to them, especially the clown with the beard, straw hat, and absurd canvas pack—and figured that they would move fast enough to pass these dinosaurs with ease.

Henry responded in kind. And raised the ante. He was annoyed because he had planned to climb the steep first pitch with just one tool, a seventy-centimeter ice ax (relatively long by modern standards), using the elegant techniques required for such tactics. This was to be his way of honoring the even greater innate elegance of the Whittlesey-Scoville ascent of 1930. Now more speed would be required, and a second tool for some moves, if we were to remain the lead party. As he approached, Henry fixed their leader with the icy stare his competitors of the early 1970s had known too well.

When I handed Henry the sharp end of the rope, I included a muttered assurance that I was familiar enough with this pitch not to require a belay if that suited his plans. He responded that, yes, he would rather like to put some distance between us and the challengers.

I have never seen the first pitch climbed faster. Henry in good form has always been a joy and an education to watch: power, precision, fluidity, flair, always in perfect control. As he disappeared over the top of the steep bulge, the rope regularly paid out. So when it came to the end, I began to climb too, moving with as much dispatch as could be marshaled with sagging canvas pack, sagging (has-been) muscles, and none too brilliant (never was) technique. It went well, though I noticed that the brim of my straw boater kept bumping against my tools when I looked down at my footing, a common problem for straw-hatted climbers, I suppose.

Somewhere along the way, the rope stopped moving briefly, so I assumed Henry had stopped to belay. Thus assured, I switched from front points to the more subtle—and precarious, for me—French technique of one-tool, ten-pointed, sidewise walking up the ice. As I thus teetered over the top of the bulge, I glanced up and observed that, no, Henry was far up the second pitch and still climbing. Hastily I skittered back onto the security of front points and two tools.

Eventually Henry fixed two ice-screw anchors at the end of the second pitch and handed me two more as I went by. I clawed up the third pitch to anchor at the base of a steep flow of beautiful bulging ice that cascaded down from the sunlight at the top of the right side of the gully. When Henry joined me, now three long rope lengths above the base, we looked down.

Far below, the ice curved out of sight beneath that bulge on the first pitch—and no other climbers yet in sight. The team of young hotshots had proved to be paper tigers. Faint sounds floated up of thrashing and bashing and desperate calls ("How much rope?" "Repeat?" "Ten feet." "What?" "Don't pull!" and the like).

### Pinnacle
### Resplendent

Henry smiled, looking relaxed and happy. He eased up the steepest part of the ice flow on the right, climbing smoothly with just one seventy-centimeter ax, emerging from shadow into brilliant sun, his silhouette against the kind of deep blue sky you seem to see only in winter in the mountains, and maybe only when looking up from the green-black depths of a dark, cold gully toward the safety and serenity and glory of the alpine gardens on Mount Washington.

When I began to climb, what a change in the spirit of the occasion! Gone was the petty competitiveness that had so rudely intruded on this day meant only for warm nostalgia and the stark beauty of the gleaming ice. Now was only affirmation, celebration. Oh, what a wondrous flow of ice had formed up there in the upper right-hand corner of the Fall of the Maiden's Tears!

As I topped out, we mused aloud on the pleasures of old climbs and old friendships, the happiness of moving up high ice in winter sunshine. But mostly our thoughts drifted back sixty years to the same lovely place, back in a different world of Sonja Henie and Hoagy Carmichael and Charles Lindbergh, when two brash Yalies and their Zenith pack and their long ice axes took on the world of cold and blowing snow and vertical ice, and thrashed their way up Huntington's crown jewel, up into the company of the mountain gods, where they remain forever in our minds.

# Interlude

# Education in Verticality:
## A Short Comedy or Farce in Four Scenes

When writing our history of technical rock and ice climbing, we faced one severe handicap. We wished to write vividly about the hardest climbs done in recent years, but our own abilities, or rather the limits of those abilities, prevented our exploring them on our own. Still, when it came to describing the most extreme ice routes in the northeastern United States, we felt that at least one of us should have personally experienced the exotic pleasures of climbing them. Fortunately, a young man named Mike Young, a superb ice climber and mountaineer, had become a close personal friend—not because we joined him on his hard routes, but for other reasons. In the interest of our research, Mike agreed to take one of us up one of the infamous climbs at Lake Willoughby in northern Vermont, locale of the longest and steepest ice in all of New England. Guy nominated Laura for this honor; Laura nominated Guy. Eventually one of us was condemned—that is, chosen. Heading off on that morning, Guy tried to keep in mind the value of direct involvement as a key to vivid writing. "At least we're not working on a history of capital punishment," he thought. The ensuing events, we decided, lent themselves less to the high drama usually associated with high-level climbing than to some sort of low farce.

**Source:** Adapted from *Yankee Rock & Ice.*

▲ ▼ ▲

THE DATE: February 7, 1981.

THE SCENE: Lake Willoughby, Vermont, which lies roughly three million miles north of anywhere warm.

DRAMATIS PERSONAE: (1) Mike Young, an ice climber of considerable attainments; (2) Guy Waterman, of considerably fewer attainments, if indeed any at all.

SCENE 1.

The two climbers are roping up at the base of more than three hundred feet of almost dead-vertical hard-frozen water ice. Wind whistles mournfully through the leafless trees in the woods below. Spindrift races fitfully across the cold surface of the ice.

WATERMAN (throwing out the rope, while looking up fearfully at the towering ramparts of frost): Say, Mike, does anybody actually fall on this stuff? I mean, do these ice screws really hold a dead-vertical drop like you could take on this?

YOUNG (abstractedly, while lacing on crampons): Oh, sure, the modern ice screw is really quite reliable. People fall a lot. No problem.

(A few minutes pass in silence, the two climbers busy with their preparations.)

WATERMAN (lacing on crampons, but evidently the idea has occurred that Young weighs approximately fifty-one pounds more than Waterman, and will be leading, of course): Uh, Mike . . . do you ever fall?

YOUNG (absorbed with sorting hardware): Huh? Oh, fall? Me? Yes. Funny thing, actually. Every season I seem to take two leader falls. Never more than two. No matter how much I climb, or how little, I always seem to manage to take two falls, and only two. Every winter. Isn't that funny?

WATERMAN (hastily): Yes, yes, funny . . .

(A few more minutes pass in silence.)

WATERMAN (a bit more softly): Uh, say, Mike . . . have you taken any falls this winter?

YOUNG (to the point): One.

WATERMAN (barely audible): Oh.

Curtain.

SCENE 2.

The second pitch. Young has executed a flawless lead of the second pitch and is now belaying at a point two-thirds of the way up the ice. Waterman is attempting to follow. Starts to fall. Actually, let's skip this scene. If you like, we could tell you about the first pitch, which went very smoothly. Curtain (quick!).

SCENE 3.

Top of the second pitch, and showing the ice a bit above that point as well. Both climbers have tied in here. Waterman is wearily handing the rack to Young, who seems unwearied in spite of the strenuous weightlifting he has just completed, having hauled a weight scarcely fifty-one pounds lighter than his own body weight up most of the second pitch.

YOUNG (with enthusiasm that Waterman finds hard to take): Wasn't that a great pitch, though?

WATERMAN (smiling weakly): Yep, wonderful!

YOUNG (gesturing upward): This next part's a whole lot easier. You won't have any trouble. It's really nice climbing. You'll love it.

WATERMAN: Yeah, wonderful!

(Waterman puts Young on belay. Young leads up about ten feet.)

YOUNG: This is lousy ice. It doesn't take the tools well at all. (Pause.) I don't think it would take ice screws either. Just flakes off.

(A further pause. Young has moved up another five feet.)

YOUNG (falling): Falling!

Curtain.

SCENE 4.

Top of the second pitch, but showing also the ice a bit below, rather than above the belay point. Young now appears approximately thirty-five feet below the spot where he appeared at the end of the previous scene. He is in a horizontal position, face up, not significantly touching the ice, swaying gently in the air, rather like a piece of scaffolding against the side of a sheer glass skyscraper. The rope, taut as a piano wire, runs from his harness up to the waist of Waterman, who is holding on for dear life.

YOUNG (shaking his head slowly): Two.

Curtain.

SHAD-
OWS
ON
THE
CLIFF

# Danger and Death on the Mountainside

The discovery of George Mallory's body still straining upward on the frozen heights of Everest after seventy-five years sent a quiver vibrating through the world of climbers. Especially older climbers. We were all brought up on the legend of 1924: drank deep from the cup of romance of "because it's there"; could not tear our imaginations' eye from the tiny figures disappearing up into the mists of the unattainable.

This was just one of many neologistic twists we learned to give the stark reality of death, that half-dreaded, half-invited angel ever brooding in the shadows of the climber's world.

Climbers (and scribblers writing about climbing) have always muddied this issue. One climber we knew, going for a graduate degree in one of those new subjects for which they give Ph.D.s in these days, shed some glaring light on this fuzzy area. Let us tell you about the odd little game he used as the basis for his academic treatise.

Our friend had heard about a study in which some researcher gave two carefully selected groups a little game of hoops and pegs. You were supposed to throw a dozen or so hoops over the pegs; you got one point for hooping the peg right in front of you and two points for the one a yard or so farther away, which wasn't easy to do. This researcher's two groups consisted of, first, a selection of entrepreneurs, risk takers in the business world, men who risked all for high stakes; and second, a control group of ordinary citizens, presumably working in staid nine-to-five jobs with regular paychecks, or otherwise economically secure. What the researcher found was that ordinary joes from the control group would regularly try at least a few throws at the farther-away peg (almost always missing, of course). The entrepreneurs, the supposed high-risk takers, would take all their hoops and stand there dropping them on the sure-thing closer peg.

Sound backward? Not if you think about it. Entrepreneurs are people who choose to put themselves in high-risk situations, with a lot to gain but also a lot to lose. Having put themselves in these situations, how do they proceed? They carefully calculate the odds in each decision and unfailingly select the safest course. They dare not indulge in wild surmises; too much is at stake. They play things out on a cold-blooded, realistic level. They have to. Only by doing so can they win the big gamble they know they've put themselves in.

We've heard that successful professional poker players are the ones who play the odds unswervingly—never drawing to an inside straight, letting their amateur opponents have fun with all those big gambles that the professional knows so rarely succeed. The cool pros never win big; they just rake in a few chips game after game.

Back to our climbing friend and those hoops and pegs. He did his thesis on a similar game, selecting a group of climbers known for their willingness to take daring leads on rock or ice, going up there high above protection on moves at the limit of their abilities. The control group was drawn from climbers who confessed to doing little leading, preferring to follow, with the rope above, never exposed to the long fall and the risk of injury or death.

As with the entrepreneurs, the lead climbers took all their hoops, dropped them all on the closest peg, then picked up their rope and climbing gear and went off to try some daring new climb. The timid followers sometimes took a few gambles with a long throw to the high-stakes peg.

The point of the story is that serious climbers know, better than almost anyone else in our sheltered modern lives, what death and dying mean. They see the dark angle on the edge of where they're going. Contrary to what the armchair world thinks, they certainly do not take stupid risks. They start by putting themselves in a very scary place—but then they coolly and deliberately calculate every move in order to come home free and safe. This is what it's all about.

Tom Patey, the marvelous Scottish climber and bon vivant, once said something to the effect that people think solo climbers are unsafe, but, on the contrary, solo climbers are *very safe.* (Having told you that, though, we have to tell you also that Tom Patey died, a young man, because of a silly little mistake on a routine rappel.)

When you read about death and dying in the mountains, think about these things. Serious, hard-core climbers do.

Here are some stories about them. In the first two the climbers are fighting to avoid their rendezvous with the dark angel. In the fictional pieces that follow, that dreaded guest has already arrived, and the survivors are struggling to deal with its inexorable presence.

# A NIGHT IN ODELL GULLY

*"There were giants in the earth in those days."*

—Genesis 6:4

**T**he following true story is based on conversations with three of the participants and on a more detailed version published in *Appalachia*. We were good friends and climbing buddies of Ed Nester, and we have often thought that possibly only Ed could have pulled off what he did here. Why? Because while a handful of other climbers were technically skilled enough to go up where he did, Ed had a stupidly stubborn streak in him that often drove us batty, but, on this occasion, allowed him to focus blindly on the single objective of keeping that other man alive, setting his teeth in defiance of all that the mountain gods, at their most vindictive, could throw at him. Anyone else would have been sensible enough to get the heck out of there. Not Ed.

**Source:** *Wilderness Ethics.*

▲ ▼ ▲

**March 24, 1968, 2:55 p.m. on a Sunday afternoon. A howling storm raged over Mount** Washington, the Northeast's highest peak. One of the country's top ice climbers of that day, Ed Nester, was having a bowl of soup with his fiancée in the Pinkham Notch Lodge at the base of Washington. They had climbed the ice on the mountain on Saturday, but the deteriorating weather that morning had led them to decide to stay off the ice, dry out, and prepare to go home. As soon as they finished their soup, they would start the long drive back to New York City.

They never finished that bowl of soup.

The telephone that connected Pinkham with a string of emergency lines up on the mountain rang. A young woman answered, then ran out the door and back in again. Nester asked her if anything had happened, hoping the answer would be reassuring. She asked him to speak to the Forest Service ranger on the telephone. High up in Huntington Ravine, the steep-sided glacial cirque whose ice-choked gullies attract ice climbers from all over the East, two ice climbers were stranded, unable to get down. While climbing in the bad weather, they had been hit by an avalanche. A third member of the party, carried lower by the avalanche, had managed to get down and send word for help.

The ranger told Nester that the two were OK, but unable to get down on their own. Could Nester come up and lead a rescue? Nester thought to himself, "If they are OK and the weather is so bad that they can't get down, how am I going to get up to them?" But he agreed to start up.

Up on the mountain, things had already started to happen. Just below the floor of Huntington Ravine is a cabin used as a base by ice climbers. It was to this cabin that the shaken climber, Donn Stahlman, had made it with the news about his stranded partners, Jeff Damp and Tom Davis. At the cabin he found another climber, Charlie Porter, who used an emergency phone to notify the Forest Service rangers, then returned to the cabin and prepared to start up himself.

Porter and Stahlman left the cabin and began trudging up through the storm toward the floor of Huntington Ravine. In minutes they were overtaken by a huge Thiokol snow machine, which took them on board and continued slowly crunching up toward the base of the ice gullies above. Also aboard were two Forest Service rangers and two employees of the Appalachian Mountain Club, which maintains the lodge down at Pinkham Notch.

By 3:20 P.M. the six men stood on the floor of Huntington Ravine. Above them towered the rocky walls of the mountain, through which several gullies wend upward, filled with deep snow for the most part, but with hard blue water ice at the steepest points. One of these gullies is known as Odell Gully (after the first man to climb it). On that particular Sunday afternoon, however, none of the gullies or any other feature could be distinguished from below. A swirling, howling storm of snow and high winds reduced visibility to a few feet. The temperature hovered at about zero, with winds gusting to seventy-five miles per hour, according to actual observations made at the Summit Observatory, some two thousand feet farther up the mountain.

From their knowledge of the Huntington terrain, the six men were able to work their way up through the storm to where the snow steepened into ice at the bottom of Odell Gully. They shouted up into the maelstrom above, but their voices were swallowed insignificantly in the shriek of the storm. Was it possible that two men were up there somewhere, still alive after sitting motionless on a precarious icy ledge for two and a half hours?

Porter and Stahlman roped up, and Porter began to lead up the ice. After one rope's length, he tied himself in and signaled for Stahlman to follow. As he climbed, Stahlman found that one ankle was weakened from the strains of his tumble in the avalanche earlier that day. He was barely able to reach the stance that Porter had chopped out on the ice slope above. As soon as he did, Porter was off again, working his way to the right edge of the gully and eventually to a niche in the side of the cliff there, which the climbers came to call "the cave."

At this point, however, Stahlman was simply unable to climb farther. Exhausted, injured, cold, and buffeted by the relentless winds and blowing ice crystals that froze on the climbers' eyelashes, tending to freeze the eyelids shut, Stahlman retreated. He descended one of their ropes to the base of the ice, where one of the Forest Service rangers escorted him down to the more sheltered floor of the ravine and eventually on down to the cabin. One of the AMC employees had already descended too.

That left one ranger and one AMC man up at the base of the ice, Charlie Porter two pitches up at the "cave," and somewhere up above there in the storm, the stranded pair, Damp and Davis. The time was 4:25 P.M. Not much daylight left.

Porter shouted up into the wind once more, and this time a faint human sound echoed back. He shouted again. Answering shouts responded through a lull in the snowy inferno. Damp and Davis were alive—and from what he could gather, Porter understood them to be not seriously injured. It was clear, however, that their condition must be deteriorating, immobilized as long as they were, without shelter on a small ledge on the steep ice, exposed to the full force of the storm. Porter shouted down to the two men at the base of the ice. By this time, though, with steeper ice above him, and very cold and tired himself from his prolonged struggled against the storm, Porter could go no farther. He rigged the ropes carefully to prepare to descend.

Meanwhile, down at Pinkham Notch, Ed Nester had gathered his equipment together and was soon aboard a second snow machine, being driven up the mountain. Somewhere near the cabin that machine broke down, and Nester continued on foot. He met two climbers coming down and asked if they knew how to do technical ice climbing. One of them said he did. "How technical?" asked Nester. "Very technical," replied the other, who turned out to be Dave Seidman, who the previous summer had made the first ascent of the South Face of Mount McKinley, a daring climb that stamped him as one of the top up-and-coming mountaineers of this country. Seidman willingly agreed to join Nester.

It is difficult to say what might have been the outcome of the story had it not been for this fortuitous linking up, on a late Sunday afternoon, of two outstanding ice climbers, Nester and Seidman. Both were to play key roles in the events of the next twelve hours.

At about 5:30 P.M. Nester and Seidman reached the base of the ice. The storm was now at its height, darkness nearly complete. The peak gust of wind officially recorded that evening on the summit was 104 miles per hour. The temperature dropped to two degrees below zero. When the rescue pair arrived, the remaining ranger, close to the edge of survival himself, immediately descended.

Nester asked Seidman if he wanted to lead. Seidman said the idea didn't overly excite him. Nester asked again, and Seidman agreed to give it a try.

The two pitches up to the cave, where Porter still huddled by himself, went fairly smoothly, despite the worsening storm. The three men exchanged information, and Porter then descended the fixed and partly frozen ropes. He and eventually everyone else in the ravine retreated to the warmth and security of the cabin below.

Up at the cave, Seidman prepared to lead the steep ice above to try to reach the stranded climbers. The storm was now so bad that Seidman shouted to Nester, "It looks hard—I'll most likely fall." Then he swung his ice ax and began to climb.

It was 8 P.M. before Seidman, calling on all the resources of a superb ice leader, reached the ledge where Damp and Davis hunched motionless. Working as quickly as the wind and cold permitted, Seidman rigged solid anchors in the ice and lowered the two climbers to the cave, then descended himself.

In the process of lowering Damp, the full extent of their predicament became clear for the first time: during the afternoon avalanche, one of Damp's crampons had stabbed into his leg, leaving a serious wound and resulting in much loss of blood. He could not put any weight on the injured leg, and wounds of that severity have a tendency to weaken the body's defenses against cold and wind chill. Lowering him over the steep pitch above the cave was possible precisely because it was steep—Seidman could simply let Damp down like a sack of frozen potatoes. Below, where the angle was less, would not be so easy.

Nevertheless, Seidman and Nester felt they had reason for optimism now that the actual rescue had begun. They were all down at the cave now. All that remained was to descend to the base of the ice and arrange for Damp to be littered down the steep snow below, to where a snow machine could take him out.

Seidman went down first, to clear the frozen ropes. When he reached the base of the ice, confident that the others would soon be down, and totally exhausted himself, he immediately set off down through the storm. It was 9 P.M. when he reached the cabin, where he told the assembled rescue teams that the others were on their way down but would need a litter for Damp from the base of the ice. He then collapsed for some badly needed and richly deserved rest. Through those early evening hours he had absorbed the maximum strain of leading difficult ice in the dark at the height of the storm, lowering the stranded pair, then clearing the frozen ropes below.

The rescue team set off from the cabin and fought their way back up in the dark and storm, hauling a toboggan-type litter. It took until 10:30 P.M. before four of them reached the base of the ice.

To their consternation, the only person there was Davis, helpless from exhaustion and cold and unable to explain where Nester and Damp might be. The rescuers got Davis up and escorted him down to the cabin. They radioed to Pinkham Notch that more technical help was needed to get to Nester and Damp.

After Seidman had left the cave, Nester had tried to lower Davis. Because of the angle of descent, however, this had not worked. Somehow Davis got back up to the cave, and Nester then rigged him up for a rappel of the frozen ropes. After more than an hour Davis finally reached the base of the ice.

The ropes above him froze solidly to the slope, however, and Nester was unable to determine whether Davis was in fact off the ropes yet or not. Furthermore, all the available ropes were now thoroughly frozen and useless for lowering Damp—and in any case the strategy had not worked for lowering the able-bodied Davis, so it clearly would be both futile and dangerous to attempt to lower the injured Damp single-handedly. Left to handle the situation by himself, with no one around to get up to him, and unable to see or hear anything of what was going on at the base of the ice, Nester evaluated his predicament. He knew that he could descend the ropes himself and find out what the problem was at the base of the ice—even, perhaps, if help were there, instruct them how to control the descent of Damp if he could get another rope to lower him with. However, if he went down he could by no means be sure of getting back up. And if he didn't get back up, Damp would surely die.

Nester decided to prepare to spend the night on the wind-racked ice ledge. He tried wrapping a lightweight rescue blanket around Damp. The wind first frustrated his efforts, then eventually tore the blanket to shreds. He cut off Damp's crampons and somehow stuffed the injured climber into a bivouac bag just big enough for one person. He then shoved him into the corner of the ice wall and lay against him to protect him further from the wind. He talked to Damp all during the night, asking him questions about school, climbing, anything to keep his consciousness engaged. In the late hours, Damp haltingly asked if he was going to make it through the night or whether he would die. Nester told him, by God, he'd better make it; what was the point of wasting this night up here for nothing?

The scene at the cave through that long night exceeds the imagination of anyone who has not seen a mountain storm in full fury.

There is a limit beyond which the human body cannot endure cold and exhaustion. When a person nears that limit, the mind will accept any rationalization to justify its own survival instinct and defend a decision to get to safety. In light of this, it is singular that Nester—having thought through the logic of descending the frozen ropes himself to see what was the matter below, but having also realized that if he did not get back up, Damp would die, having that rationalization full in front of him—nevertheless determined to stay up there in that storm and risk his own life, not just in a single moment, but through a long and punishing night, to save the life of a climber he'd never met before.

If there has been a clearer example of sheer personal heroism, we've never heard of it.

Dimly aware of the precarious predicament of the stranded pair, the rescuers who brought back Davis had called for additional technical support. Charlie Porter, who had been sleeping soundly after his own great efforts earlier that day, was roused. Another climber was located at Pinkham. It was 1 o'clock in the morning before the two were taken up the mountain in the snow machine. Once in the darkened, storm-swept ravine, they found that all trace of tracks had been blown away. This resulted in their heading first into the wrong gully. By the time they reached the base of the ice in Odell, it was 4 A.M.

Now, finally, the storm had begun to abate. With the wind less noisy, their loud calls were heard and answered by Nester. Incredibly, Nester and Damp were still alive up there. Porter and the other climber, George Smith, began the ascent. The beginning of daylight soon assisted their labors. They rigged a well-anchored system for lowering Nester and Damp on the same rope, Nester guiding the helpless, injured man's descent. At the base of the ice a further handicap was added when overeager support rescuers let the toboggan-litter get away from them, to slide uselessly 1,000 feet down the mountain, empty. Nester set up a brake-bar system using his ice ax, then lowered Damp's recumbent form down the long snow slope, supported on either side by other rescuers. Eventually they got down to where the snow machine could pick up the victim and take him down the long mountain trail to a waiting ambulance.

Above, Porter and Smith retrieved ropes and gear and lingered to watch the dawn of a lovely day. "In fact," recalled Smith, "this was the best winter morning I had ever seen."

That Damp and his friends recovered completely from the night in Odell

Gully was nothing short of a miracle—a miracle with names like Ed Nester, Dave Seidman, and Charlie Porter. The mountain gods, having shrieked so pitilessly all night, in the end relented.

But the mountain gods are fickle. They respect no heroes. Scarcely more than a year later, an enormous avalanche rushed blindly down Dhaulagiri, halfway around the world in the Himalaya, and buried seven men, among them Dave Seidman. A few summers after that, during a descent from a difficult route in the Canadian Rockies, a rappel anchor pulled loose and sent another climber to his death on the glacier below—Ed Nester.

Those two names, however, will always be associated in honor for what they did more than a quarter century ago, on a night in Odell Gully.

# WINTER ABOVE TREE LINE

**W**hen we first met each other, this epic fiasco had just occurred, in the winter of 1968–1969. That should have tipped off Laura that Guy was totally out of his mind. But it didn't work that way. Instead, she urged him to retell the story so many times he eventually wrote it down. It finally made it into print in *New England Outdoors* magazine in 1977; and later in the first edition of *Backwoods Ethics* (1979); and again in *Wilderness Ethics* (1993). Reprints have been distributed in several winter climbing instructional courses over the years, to serve as the ultimate "horrible example" of all the wrong moves in winter climbing. You'll get to read about it again, serving as another kind of example, in our chapter called "Five Winter Trips."

▲ ▼ ▲

**This is a tale that almost became a tragedy.**

It's about the brutal cruelty of the mountain gods in wintertime—though on this occasion they chose to spare their helpless victims, perhaps to see if they could profit from the experience.

It's a story worth retelling for the lessons it teaches about winter camping and climbing in New England's mountains.

The day after Christmas 1968, a father and his sixteen-year-old son started on a trek through New Hampshire's White Mountains by struggling into huge packs and snowshoes and slowly plodding through a couple of feet of fresh snow up a mountain trail called the Valley Way. Whoever named this trail had the terminology on backward: the "Valley" Way climbs nearly four thousand vertical feet in less than four miles, up into the northern end of the Presidential Range.

Their objective was to traverse the peaks of the Presidentials and, if possible, to continue on across other mountain ranges to the west. They never got near those western ranges. The Presidentials taught them several lessons, which we'll try to enumerate as the story goes along.

Father and son got about three miles that first day. Besides a late start, their packs were jammed full of enough winter equipment and food to last them ten days, and this was before the day of much lightweight gear. The packs weighed more than eighty pounds apiece. The fresh, unconsolidated December snow conditions, plus the weight of those packs, meant that at every step the lead man sank in about two feet. It was absurdly slow going.

▲ ▼ ▲

**Lesson 1: Don't count on moving rapidly in winter.** Trail conditions can make half a mile per hour an exhausting speed. The Appalachian Mountain Club suggests, "Guidebook travel times should be doubled in winter." Under some conditions, that advice is not nearly conservative enough.

▲ ▼ ▲

That night, they camped right on one of the few level spots in the trail and watched the temperature sink to the nether regions. Nearby Mount Washington, where there's a functioning weather observatory, broke all records for that date with a reading of thirty-two degrees below zero. But so far they were doing OK, and the next day they continued successfully until they emerged above tree line in the Presidential Range in the high col between Mounts Adams and Madison.

Here the full fury of a notorious Presidentials winter was tuning up. Winds shrieked and howled, buffeting the two climbers at every step. Temperatures below zero in a still valley feel darn cold; those same temperatures on an exposed, wind-racked ridge are of an entirely new order of cold.

A curious feature of the Presidentials in winter is that much of the alpine zone has relatively little snow on the ground. That is due to those ferocious winds, which blow most of it clean off the treeless heights, leaving a frozen terrain of rocks, ice, and very hard-packed snow. Where wind currents permit snow to collect, occasional vast snowfields build up to considerable depth, covering every feature of the mountain and every trace of the trail. Aside from these great snowfields, though, New England's most wintry winter spot paradoxically does not have very deep snow.

Father and son came prepared for this environment. They changed snowshoes for crampons. They pulled windproof nylon pants over their regular wool pants. They donned face masks, around which parka hoods were pulled tight, and "monster mitts" that extended up to their elbows. No flesh must be left to that punishing wind.

▲  ▼  ▲

**Lesson 2: Bring clothing suitable for full-scale arctic conditions.** Especially important is adequate headgear (because so much heat loss occurs through the head), genuine winter boots (not summer-weight hiking boots), and a good mitten-glove combination.

▲  ▼  ▲

Our two climbers managed to reach the two nearest summits, Mounts Madison and Adams, by leaving their heavy packs lower down on the ridge and dashing up to the summit and back with just ice ax in hand. The air was crystal clear, and the sky an unbelievably deep blue, so they had no difficulty in finding their packs again each time they came back down from the summits, a fact they were to recall with grim irony twenty-four hours later.

That night they reached the col between Mounts Adams and Jefferson, where they huddled into a small emergency shelter that was maintained there by the Forest Service.

In the morning the temperature had risen to twelve degrees above zero. Visibility was socked in and light snow was falling, but the wind wasn't knocking them off their feet anymore, so they made the decision to proceed. Their trail was to slab the broad shoulder of Mount Washington, the largest peak in the Northeast.

The decision to move on in those conditions proved to be a dangerous mistake. Visibility was soon no more then fifty feet. Furthermore, it became obvious they had underestimated how much wind they would be dealing with as they moved out of the col. They had scarcely started when it became evident that a full-blown winter storm was under way.

Climbing out of the col onto the side of Jefferson proved to be hard work under those conditions. Laboring under heavy packs, they became quite warm and shed their wool shirts from under their wind parkas. The father decided that uncovering his pack to stow the shirt inside would risk frostbite to his fingers, so he just tucked the shirt securely under the top flap and resumed the arduous climb.

As they rounded the shoulder of Jefferson, they began to traverse one of those huge snowfields that collect on the Presidentials in winter. (This snowfield is visible from the highway well into July most years, so its depth in midwinter is obviously considerable. In fact, it covers almost every cairn or other trace on the trail.)

With low visibility, it became difficult for the two climbers to stay on trail. Then, as they came out of the lee of the summit, the full fury of the wind slammed into them, blowing a steady torrent of ice crystals into their faces. Progress became painfully slow. To guard against losing their way—which could have been disastrous—the son would go out from the last identified cairn as far as he could while keeping it in view. Then the father would go out from there as far as he could without losing sight of the son, and stand there waiting for some brief lapse in the wind to try to squint forward into the fury of the storm in a forlorn effort to find another cairn. In all that snow, however, only the tops of the tallest cairns showed, and often many minutes passed before they could spot the next one and move on.

To one who has not been up there, it is difficult to convey the full import of a winter storm above tree line. The myriad unfamiliar experiences and sensations include:

▲ Barely being able to stand on your feet, braced always by your ice ax, and moving forward fitfully only between gusts.

▲ The unrelenting din and tumult of the wind, so loud that you must shout virtually into your companion's ear to be heard.

▲ The featureless, enigmatic whiteness created by the unrelieved snow, ice crystals, and clouds, which surround you on all sides, up and down.

▲ The sense of every little procedure being enormously difficult and time-consuming. (Even looking at your watch, for example, involves uncovering the wrist from the monster mitt, parka, and shirt, then painstakingly getting them all snugly back together. It perhaps shouldn't take so long to do, but up there it does.)

All of these sensations are exciting enough if you step out into them for a half hour. If you're out in them for several hours, they'll wear you down. If you're out in them all day long, with no prospect of escaping them at night save in a tiny tent somehow staked up there, you have to learn to take it as a way of life.

Admiral Byrd, caught in an Antarctic blizzard, described it in *Alone* as "extravagantly insensate":

> Its vindictiveness cannot be measured on an anemometer sheet. It is more than just wind: it is a solid wall of snow moving at gale force, pounding like surf. The whole malevolent rush is concentrated upon you as upon a personal enemy. In the senseless explosion of sound you are reduced to a crawling thing on the margin of a disintegrating world; you can't see, you can't hear, you can hardly move.

▲ ▼ ▲

It is this scene that the jealous winter gods of Mount Washington aspire to imitate. Sometimes they do a pretty good job.

Eventually the father and son did get across the snowfield and out onto the southern slopes of Mount Jefferson, where once again they could stumble on blown-clear rocks and ice, where cairns were at least visible from time to time, when the wind-driven ice would permit them to steal a look ahead.

▲ ▼ ▲

**Lesson 3: Never try to move in a full-scale storm above tree line.** These two should have stayed put in their shelter for a day, as they were to do in an even greater storm later. No one should risk becoming exhausted or lost in a snowfield in the incredible and relentless fury of those White Mountain storms.

▲ ▼ ▲

When they got to the far side of Jefferson, the cloud cover momentarily lifted, revealing a gentle slope angling up to the summit of Jefferson. The two climbers could not resist the lure of the summit. They had already bagged Madison and Adams; they had to grab Jefferson while they had the chance. Dropping their packs, they decided on a quick rush up to the nearly visible summit and back to their packs.

The climb went easily, and they delighted in the freedom of an easy dash uphill without packs and with the wind at their backs. When they landed on the summit and congratulated each other, the Mountain King stopped smiling and frowned.

The clouds came down again; the wind picked up. Father and son suddenly realized they could not see more than a few feet, that they had lost all sense of which direction they had come up from and which direction to descend, that the wind-driven snow had completely obliterated all trace of their tracks in a matter of minutes, that each rocky outcropping on the mountain looked like all the others, and that—the crushing blow—the father's compass, which he always carried handy in his wool shirt pocket, was still there, in the wool shirt that he had so carefully tucked in the pack, which now lay on the trail somewhere below them.

How can you be lost when you know just where you are (in this case, the very summit of Mount Jefferson, at 5,715 feet, in a howling, screaming, swirling thicket of fog and driven ice crystals)? For several minutes the two tried to remain calm and move about the summit slowly, trying vainly to get some sense of which way anything lay. Calm and rational discussion is difficult when to make yourself heard you must stand right up against the other person's ear and bellow at the top of your lungs.

At length, they agreed on their best guess as to the way down and resolutely plodded ahead. After an eternity, repeatedly suppressing fears that they might be going in the wrong direction, they were overjoyed to see one of the cairns for the trail they had been on before. But when they arrived there, they soon figured out that they were back on the north side of the mountain—which meant that in their careful calculations as to which way to descend from the summit, they had been precisely 180 degrees off course.

Now they once again had to face the risks and difficulties of crossing that same snowfield. Their tracks were, of course, long since wiped out in the wind-driven snow. Furthermore, the wind had increased considerably, the snow lay deeper (covering more of the cairns), and they were much,

much more tired after all the buffeting they had already taken at the hands of the storm. They did manage somehow to swim or sink or wade or flounder across the snowfield. Finally, out of the implacably swirling cloud and snow, they once again saw ahead of them on the trail their packs, now encrusted with snow and ice.

▲  ▼  ▲

**Lesson 4: Never go anywhere without a compass.** It is hard to imagine getting turned around 180 degrees on a familiar summit, but it happened in this case and it can happen again. Once you lose that all-important sense of the direction of things, that alpine world up there suddenly appears featureless and inscrutable—and totally hostile. Without a compass, you're dead lost, body and soul.

▲  ▼  ▲

**Lesson 5: Don't count on following your own footprints.** The wind can blow them to oblivion in a minute or two. The hole left by an ice ax lasts somewhat longer, so look for those rather than your crampon tracks— but nothing lasts long in a serious Presidentials gale.

▲  ▼  ▲

**Lesson 6: Never separate yourself from the equipment you require for survival.** These two reckless but lucky adventurers eventually found their packs again before they were overcome by fatigue, darkness, or just plain inability to find their way in the storm. Without their packs—and spare clothes, sleeping bags, tent, stove, and food—they would surely have perished in the open. With their packs, their chances of at least surviving were considerably improved.

▲  ▼  ▲

All of these exhausting perambulations not only left both father and son fatigued, but also consumed a considerable part of the available daylight hours. It soon became clear to them that they had neither strength nor daylight left in which to climb the enormous summit cone of Mount Washington—more than one thousand feet of elevation—on which the fury of the wind would certainly increase.

▲ ▼ ▲

**Lesson 7: Remember that early winter days have the fewest daylight hours.** As Yogi Berra said, it's the time of year when it gets late early. This fact should be kept in mind in all winter trip planning.

▲ ▼ ▲

The prospect now confronted them of trying to set up a camp in which they could survive a night immobilized in this awesome storm. Having come this far, they were now many miles of formidable mountain terrain from any trail that led down out of the alpine zone to a nearby road. The only trail near them was the Sphinx Trail, which led sharply down into a vast wilderness area known as the Great Gulf, through which they would have to lug themselves and their enormous packs for many miles, in several feet of unbroken, unconsolidated snow, the depth of which must have considerably increased during the storm. That course could probably not be done in one day, and in any case would mean a total defeat to their plans, and perhaps two hard days of dispirited plodding through the woods to safety.

So they felt themselves strongly committed to sticking out the storm. Perhaps it would die down during that night and the morning. (Mountaineers tend to be ridiculously optimistic when all nature is screaming evil tidings at them.) They noticed that at least the temperature felt warmer, and mistakenly took that to be an encouraging factor.

Dropping a bit below the crest of the ridge, they carefully selected a spot in the lee of some large rock outcroppings, where they laboriously leveled a site for the tent. As they got the tent up, they noticed that the snow had changed texture—in fact, it was more like sleet or freezing rain. The temperature had indeed climbed, but that meant trouble, not relief.

They managed to get set up inside the tent just before darkness. Then the wind shifted. That night proved even more frightening than the day out there on the snowfield. The wind repeatedly swelled into great buffeting blows, at which the helpless inmates of the tent would grab its A-frame poles, trying to hold it together against the force of the tempest, wondering how long the fabric would hold up against this punishment. Fortunately it did last through the night, but just barely.

In between the worst gusts of the storm, the father spent a full hour methodically scraping the encrusted ice and snow off his wool shirt, which had sat exposed on the outside of his pack during the day. He correctly reasoned that it would be vital to survival, since down garments lose their value as they get wet, and thus the time spent cleaning the ice off his shirt was a good investment. But the price of lost sleep was a stiff one to pay.

▲ ▼ ▲

**Lesson 8: Always take the time to pack essential items properly.** In this case the price was only lost sleep. In other cases failure to stash an item inside your pack can result in its becoming so soaked as to be useless for the rest of the trip, or at the worst it can be torn off the pack unnoticed and turn up missing when it's needed.

▲ ▼ ▲

Early the next morning, the wind finally wore down the battered tent. Shortly after daylight, a brief but unmistakable ripping sound announced that the outer fly had given way. Within seconds, it was reduced to tattered shreds flopping noisily at the downwind end. Father and son knew that it was an unnecessary question to ask how long the main fabric of the tent might hold out.

▲ ▼ ▲

**Lesson 9: In setting up a tent, never assume that the current wind direction will necessarily hold constant.** As a matter of fact, it is tempting to make the generalization that no tent made can stand up to the fury of a Presidentials storm at its worst. You're better off not putting your confidence in any above-tree-line shelter if you have no easy escape route. Snow caves or igloos offer a better chance for survival, but they are time-consuming to erect, can get you very wet in the process, and cost daylight hours that can probably be better spent getting to some less exposed spot, preferably below tree line.

Somehow father and son got their tent dismantled and set off desperately to get down out of the wind. The Sphinx Trail proved extremely steep and difficult to negotiate with their gigantic packs. Between the time it took them to pack up, the difficulty of descent, and the formidably deep, soft snow they encountered down in the woods, they made very few miles that day, and stopped for the night at one of the shelters that have since been removed from the Great Gulf Wilderness. By nightfall, the storm had abated. It stopped sleeting—but this only brought a new danger. All of their clothes had become wet, and now the temperature again began to drop.

▲ ▼ ▲

**Lesson 10: In winter, neither wind nor cold is as deadly an enemy as warmth and rain, followed by cold.** When a winter storm turns warm and drops rain, that's the time to look out for your life. You'd better be prepared to get out of the mountains fast, especially if your clothes and other essential equipment have been getting wet. A sudden drop in temperature after a freezing rain can catch you with your defenses down.

▲ ▼ ▲

As it was, this father and son spent their worst night yet shivering in down sleeping bags that had lost most of their insulating warmth from the soaking they had received. Both wore all of their clothes, but those big fluffy down jackets that had felt so warm a few days earlier now clung damp and clammy.

▲ ▼ ▲

**Lesson 11: Many layers of wool are worth more than the finest down gear when wetness is a potential problem.** It's a mountaineer's cliché that wool is "warm even when wet." Most experienced climbers place little reliance on those big down parkas you see in the ads. Newer fabrics now in widespread use have proven to be even more mountain-worthy. But this was 1968. And it remains true that layers of sweaters, shirts, and underwear, whether of wool or the newer fabrics, are far more reliable than one monster parka when the chips are down.

▲ ▼ ▲

Somehow they shivered through that night. The whole next day was spent in a dreary plod through bottomless soft snow, laboring under huge packs, oppressed additionally by the sense of having been totally defeated by the casual fury of what was only a typical period of bad weather in the Presidentials.

The foolish pair didn't know when to give up. After spending a morning in a Laundromat, repeatedly dropping dimes (this was more than a quarter century ago!) in the dryers until their sleeping bags and clothes were fluffy again, they set off at noon the very next day to climb directly up Mount Washington, this time using the eight-mile summer auto road for their route of ascent.

Along that road, where it rises above tree line, there were then, at half-mile intervals, a series of boxes for the emergency refuge of the summit weather observers on their trips up and down. Each one was roughly a cube, seven feet each way on the inside with one double door for access and one double window for light. They were, needless to say, extremely well secured to the mountainside. These days the weather observers almost always ride up and down in a fancy snow machine, so the romance of risky foot travel is gone—and so are those emergency boxes.

Our intrepid pair reached one of those boxes at fifty-five hundred feet on that afternoon of December 31. They did not leave it until January 3.

What happened was another storm, this one seemingly designed to make the earlier one look like a faint breeze. For three nights and two days it was unthinkable to move on the mountain. The summit weather observatory recorded winds of more than 100 miles per hour for twenty-three straight hours at one point, with peak gusts well over 150. The temperature dropped to twenty-six degrees below zero on January 1, ranged between eleven below and eighteen below on January 2, and warmed up to a mild-three below on January 3.

Inside the box, father and son were far better off than in the previous storm, having learned to stay put. When they started their stove for a meal, the indoor temperature even got above zero (although never above ten degrees). They lived inside their down sleeping bags.

Their biggest problem, besides boredom, was getting snow to melt for water. Any loose snow had long since been blown off into the next county. To get snow, one of the two would get dressed in full climbing regalia, including face mask, monster mitts, and crampons. Then the other would open the doors, and the first would hop out and wrestle the outer door closed while the second slammed the inner one shut. Ice ax in hand, the person outside would creep up the slope to where a cornice of hard-packed snow had accumulated nearby. There he would spread open a stuff sack, holding it open with one knee and one hand. Then he would strike the cornice repeatedly with his ice ax. At each blow, chunks of snow would dislodge and immediately be picked up and shot off by the wind—but some of them might land in the stuff sack. This process would be repeated until enough of the precious snow had accumulated in the bag to satisfy their water requirements for the day. Then the wary and frozen climber would creep back to the box, knock hard on the door, and jump inside. The next half hour would be devoted to assiduously sweeping snow off sleeping bags and everything else, since opening the doors for even those spit seconds resulted in filling the box with a thin coating of spindrift over everything. It was, of course, vital not to allow the snow to stay on the sleeping bags, where it might melt into and soak the down.

Boredom was combated principally by resorting to the reading matter brought along in anticipation of the prospect of being pinned down like this. The son made out all right with some dime-store mystery stories. The father had made the mistake of bringing Dostoevsky's *Notes from the Underground* and a poetical translation of *The Iliad*. Such heavy stuff had absolutely no appeal in these surroundings and went unread.

▲ ▼ ▲

**Lesson 12: Sex and violence are the only reading matter able to command attention at fifty-five hundred feet in a howling tempest.** Can the culture.

▲ ▼ ▲

They also ripped out the last fifty-two pages of a small memo pad and made an impromptu deck of cards. In the ensuing poker games, each used his precious lunch and snack items for chips. This resulted in a deadly serious game. When you are staking your last best candy bar on three nines, you've got to be sure they're winners! Even a small hard candy must have the support of a pair of face cards at the least.

On January 3, with the wind easing off to something in the general neighborhood of fifty miles per hour, they managed to leave their box and struggle to the summit and back, later descending back down the road, much subdued and humbled by their vacation in the mountains.

Those two were lucky. They survived all their mistakes and inexperience. Others have been less fortunate.

▲ ▼ ▲

**Lesson 13: Never trifle with winter in the mountains.** If you decide to undertake this special madness called winter climbing, prepare yourself well. Read up about it, get the correct equipment, but, most important of all, hook up with someone who has experience in that unique world. Start slowly, with day trips only at first, then with plenty of overnight experience below tree line, where you can learn to deal with the cold without the additional devastating problem of wind.

▲ ▼ ▲

It's not just that the wind feels stronger and colder in winter. It *is* stronger. The average wind speed on Mount Washington in July is 24.7 miles per hour; in January it's 43.8. From 1948 to 1975, the fastest wind recorded during July averaged 80.7 miles per hour; during January it was 124.9.

Everybody knows where winds like these take you on those famous "wind chill" charts.

To repeat, the wisest procedure is to learn directly from more experienced climbing partners. Clubs like the Appalachian Mountain Club in the White Mountains, the Green Mountain Club in Vermont, and the Adirondack Mountain Club in New York state have organized programs for helping novices gain experience under counsel from those who have been through it all.

Above all, try to avoid the mistakes we've outlined above, which that foolish father and son encountered many years ago.

You can profit from mistakes, as they did. The son in our story went on to become an outstanding mountain climber, with first ascents in the Canadian Rockies and Alaska, including the East Ridge of Mount Huntington, the South Face of Mount Hunter, and the redoubtable six-thousand-foot Southeast Spur of Hunter, all climbs of exceptional difficulty. The father went on to many more years of pleasurable winter climbing in the hills of New England, and wound up co-authoring this book with his wife, Laura Waterman.

# MOUNT EVEREST AND THE BRONX PLUMBER

## A STORY

by Guy Waterman

This tale grew out of our fascination with the early Everest sagas. Those larger-than-life tiny figures straining upward, forever upward, forever unsuccessful, formed a background and set a tone for many of our generation's vision of climbing, albeit superimposed on our diminutive New England landscape. The striving is inseparable from climbing mountains, no matter how inconsequential. Perhaps that is the theme of this entire collection. This story was Guy's first piece of published fiction.

**Source:** The October 1976 issue of *Off Belay*.

▲ ▼ ▲

**Strictly an armchair mountain climber, that's me. You'd never catch me up there** dangling from a clothesline. I have one cardinal principle about all forms of exercise: if I feel the urge to get up and do something physical, I go lie down quietly until that urge leaves me completely.

I do enjoy reading about mountaineering, though. Especially the old Everest sagas. What great romances those struggles were, back in the 1920s and 1930s, when Tibet was unknown and Nepal forbidden. What great heroes those old-time climbers were . . . Mallory and Irvine . . . Colonel Norton . . . Shipton and Tilman. Frank Smythe at Camp Six . . . Odell alone at twenty-five thousand feet straining through the mists for one more sight of his friends above . . . General Bruce. Those were the days when men were men.

If I hadn't been familiar with this literature of early Everest, I might never have stumbled onto a most amazing discovery. That's what my story is about. The reader will not want to believe it really happened; I have trouble believing it myself.

You see, I've never had the slightest interest in spiritualism or all that bunk about contacting spirits from another world. When a man dies, he's over with, I've always believed. Your body goes a-moldering in the grave, and when the worms are through with you, that's it. The old Hindoo notion about transmigration of souls from one body to another, that's a lot of hooey, right? Right! Only you read my story and then tell me how you explain what I know happened to me right there in twentieth-century New York state.

I'm an ex-newspaperman, worked for one of the Big City's dailies that went under during the 1960s. When I found myself pounding the pavement, I decided to freelance it for a while. Through the death of an otherwise not very wealthy relative, it was my good fortune to inherit some country property up the Hudson River a ways, and the little villa that went with it proved a great place to get away from New York contracts and do my writing. So that's where I used to spend three days a week pounding the typewriter, trying to write something that someone somewhere would buy.

This country place is where the strange event occurred. It was a pleasant old seven-room house, with atmosphere all over it of nineteenth-century fine living. But decadent! A frightful expense, with wiring that must have been put in by Edison's father and plumbing that leaked like a fishnet out of water. I paid the bills because it sure was a great retreat, not only for my writing, but for some great weekend parties as well, where me and my friends could play at Gatsby on a modest scale.

The view from the back lawn of this old place was stunning—and turned out to have a considerable role in the events of my narrative. It looked out over the broad Hudson at exactly that point where the big river leaves the flat upstate farmland and abruptly cuts its way through the Hudson Highlands, with Storm King rising thirteen hundred feet right out of the water on the west and an even more spectacular cliff called Breakneck Ridge directly across the river. This Breakneck cliff starts right out with a beetling black precipice of six hundred feet or so, overhanging most of the way, and then merges into a wild broken ridge that rises in a series of what I think you call "false summits" until it is eventually higher than mighty Storm King across the river.

I've seen rock climbers on Breakneck Ridge. With a glass you can usually make them out from my back lawn, except that the glass in my hands and those of my friends isn't usually the kind that aids vision, but rather blurs it. Don't get me wrong now: the events that I'm going to describe happened when I was cold sober, or mostly so at any rate.

As I mentioned, the old house that looks out on this great mountain scenery—maybe unparalleled in the East—was a maintenance man's nightmare, and the old antediluvian plumbing was the immediate cause of the events that unfolded.

There was just one bathroom in the place, but it was the sort of room that Sir Thomas Crapper probably envisioned as the proper setting for his invention. Not one of your modern little two-by-four johns, but a full-size room, high-ceilinged, probably a bedroom in the days when the outhouse served those needs, with a couple of tall windows and a long walk from commode to sink, and lots of room for exercise.

I mention this particular room in such lavish detail, not because of any Freudian hang-ups, but because it played a mischievous role in the unusual events of my tale.

It all started with a Harvard-Yale football weekend. As a loyal son of Eli I had graciously extended an invitation to two misguided disciples of John Harvard, plus another Yalie, plus wives/girlfriends of the four of us, to begin with a Friday-night social at my country place, drive over for the Big Game at New Haven on Saturday, back to my place for a Big Night on Saturday night, with rest and recuperation on Sunday. After this Rabelaisian program had run its course, during which much wine had flowed and other high spirits, I discovered on Monday morning that this Paleolithic john had water all over the floor (fortunately, mostly water). The worthy apparatus was clogged,

and an effort to flush it merely added another few gallons to the rising water level on the floor.

I had not, until this occasion, needed the services of a plumber in the
small town where my villa was located, but I had discovered before that
locating tradesmen was not always easy. I was not too surprised, therefore,
that the one local plumber was on vacation. Time-consuming efforts on the
telephone eventually established the name and number of another artist of
the water pipes in the neighboring town, but he proved to have entered the
hospital on the evening before for a stay of undefined duration. I repaired
back upstairs to my little lake and made what efforts I could to poke around
at the insides of the source of the problem. These efforts availed me nothing but dirty hands, wet shoes, and a sour disposition.

It was this extremity that caused me to dial all the way back to the Bronx,
where in many long years of a workaday existence I had lived in and still
maintained a small apartment and some reliable contacts for services such
as plumbing. Even here the regular man was on vacation, but I did manage
to be referred to a certain Giovanni Malvolio, a master of the pipes who I
was assured was reliable and available. And expensive. Especially when he
had to be induced to drive all the way out from the Bronx for this one job.
But I was rather desperate for the use of my john.

These are the humble events that were the proximate cause of Mr.
Malvolio coming into my life and this story. When he drove his old muddy
Dodge truck into my driveway, I was certainly glad to anticipate the solu-
tion of my leaky toilet, but had no idea of what other astounding develop-
ments were to grow out of this seemingly routine visit.

Mr. Giovanni Malvolio showed nothing unusual in his physical presence:
he was a Bronx plumber. That about says it. On the short side, olive-skinned,
balding, slightly overweight and sloppy about the waist, an effect heightened
by the tendency of his shirt and undershirt to come loose from the trousers
they had once been tucked into. His face showed all the boredom and ab-
sence of excitement that one might expect in the life of a Bronx plumber. I
should guess his age in the neighborhood of fifty years.

This Machiavelli of the pipes dedicated his worthy efforts to wielding the
Stilson wrench for a couple of hours, while I took advantage of a spectacu-
larly clear day to work outside on my patio on a card table and typewriter.
The views of the Hudson and the precipitous highland cliffs on either side

of it were exceptionally clear and compelling, though more of a distraction than an inspiration to my literary efforts of the morning.

At length, the dumpy olive figure of Malvolio presented itself to report the reason of the problems. In fact, he bore in his grimy hand the villain of the piece, the limp, crumpled form of a once-proud Yale football pennant. Evidently, one of my Harvard friends, at an advanced hour of our Saturday-night revels, his humor somewhat warped by what others of us had regarded as an altogether satisfactory outcome of the events that afternoon (i.e., Yale won), had chosen to vent his frustration down the john, where it had succeeded in negotiating the rapids only as far as the first turn of the pipes, when it had come around and formed a barrier reef past which, after a flush or two, nothing penetrated. The Army Corps of Engineers never reduced a free-flowing stream to still waters more convincingly. I'm sure you're wondering if it is absolutely necessary for me to give you this complete picture of the fate of my unfortunate plumbing. It isn't, of course. What is of interest is Mr. Malvolio's strange conduct after the first minute or two of reporting what the trouble was and how he had successfully restored the waters to their normal, happy, free-flowing navigability.

At first, with all the sensitivity one would expect of a Bronx plumber, he had taken no notice of the sweeping beauty of natural landscape before him. When our business was mostly done, however, his eyes wandered to the river, and the cliffs and ridges beyond. Then a strange thing happened. His conversation drifted off and his gaze fixed unblinkingly on the arching silhouette of the rising mountain ridge, with the steep drop-off below. He was not excited or tense, but rather almost sleepy and in a dream state.

My first reaction was to take this as the edifying effect of such a lovely landscape on the repressed soul of a city dweller, and I commented pleasantly, "Isn't that a delightful view?"

His answer puzzled me, though I first thought nothing much of it. He said, "After that second step, I knew it would all be easy going to the top. I told Norton."

Now, these words obviously didn't make much sense coming from a dumpy, balding Bronx plumber, who had apparently never seen a mountain ridge before, and who was standing on my patio with a Stilson wrench in one grimy hand and a limp Yale banner in the other. They didn't make any sense to me either and I blurted out, "How's that again?"

His trancelike gaze at the mountain horizon seemed to be broken by the intrusion of my simple question. Malvolio jerked as if waking from a doze and looked at me blankly for a second; then his eyes blinked and his pudgy face took on again the dull, spiritless look of the Bronx, and he repeated, as if in answer to my question, something about the fate of the upstairs pipes. At this time, the import of his unusual behavior and words of the moment before had not fully penetrated to me, so I failed to press the point and our business was soon concluded. Mr. Malvolio and his truck were gone, presumably the last time I would see this gentleman with whom I had so little in common.

However, when I tried to resume my writing, I found myself thinking about the odd behavior of my Bronx pipe master. After a couple of false starts on the work I had been doing, I took a fresh sheet of paper and tried to recall the words that had so incongruously come from that dumpy form. I think I got them down correctly: "After that second step, I knew it would all be easy going to the top. I told Norton."

As a mountain climber, you'll attach these words to the Everest legend more quickly than I did at the time. At first I was completely mystified, but as I sat staring at the typed words, it did come back to me from my readings on the old 1920s expeditions. The problem high on the northeast ridge that confronted the early Everesters was regularly referred to as the "Second Step." It was this band of rock that had turned aside the attempt of Colonel Norton, forcing him out on the face, where he laboriously worked his way to what stood as an altitude record for nearly thirty years, about twenty-eight thousand feet, where a difficult couloir turned him back. It was also this Second Step that Mallory and his partner, Irvine, intended to climb directly so as to reach what appeared to be easier ground on the ridge itself and perhaps be able to go to the summit with no further technical difficulties. It was presumed to be on the rock of the Second Step that N. E. Odell caught the last glimpse of Mallory and Irvine before the mists closed in; the now-legendary pair were never seen again.

When my mind recalled all this, I rather jumped with surprise. But also with considerable confusion. What on earth was a city-bound Bronx plumber doing mumbling nonsense about a "second step" and "Norton"? Was he secretly a fan of mountain climbing? Had he got hold of the Everest literature and somehow got to thinking about it during our conversation? All explanations seemed contrived, but I was inclined to let the matter go, with a smile at the unorthodoxy of an unlettered plumber, whom one might have suspected of reading only comic books, working his way through the exotic adventures of British gentlemen in far-off Tibet half a century ago.

I mostly dismissed the whole business from my mind and might never have pursued it to its bizarre conclusion had my archaic second-floor john continued to function as Malvolio had assured me it would. However, fate (and nineteenth-century pipes) intervened. Less than a month later, the waters backed up again. Again my own efforts proved singularly ineffective.

Disgusted, I started to look up the number of the local plumber when I recalled the amusing little figure of my Bronx friend and the strange words he had uttered, and I was just curious enough to decide to pay the extra cost of getting him out for the job again. It cost me not only more money but more delay, as he was reluctant to come at all and only agreed to work me in three days hence when he could schedule the long drive out to my country escape. But he did come, and this time even stranger events unfolded.

While he was working on the pipes, sprawled out with his wrench behind and under the antiquated geometry of the reluctant john, I recalled the words he had spoken on the earlier trip and, somewhat casually, asked him if he was interested in Everest. He repeated the words blankly once, then said, "You mean Everett? I do some work for Harold Everett over on Grand Avenue. You know him?"

No, no, I remonstrated, I meant the mountain Everest. I gathered he was a fan of the old books about climbing Mount Everest. This time I really drew nothing. There was a long silence while he wrenched away at a pipe, then he slid out and wiped his hands slowly and seemed to have forgotten my question. Before he plunged back in with a new piece of equipment, I tried again. "You like to read about the early attempts to climb Mount Everest?"

He looked at me as if I was not only interrupting his concentration on the job at hand, but was mighty strange at that. No, he didn't know anything about that. Apparently he hadn't even heard of Everest, or at least didn't recall that there was such a place. He didn't know anything about mountains and he didn't have time to read, he said. I tried just once more. "Then who's Norton?" "Norton?" he repeated blankly. "Morton operates a bakery on Grand just one block up from Everett. Do you mean him?" Obviously the world of Mr. Malvolio was constrained within limits that did not include the windswept heights of the northeast ridge. Defeated, I repaired to my typewriter out on the patio and tried to resume work.

This time when Mr. Malvolio found me to report his successful repair work, I may have been a bit curt in my manner; I suppose I was covering my embarrassment at asking apparently silly questions. In any case, my Bronx friend responded to my shortness with surliness on his part, but while being careful to avoid doing me the courtesy of looking at me during what would have been an extremely brief exchange, his eyes once again lit on the rocky ramparts so foreign to his usual urban vistas. Once again his whole manner altered. His voice trailed off, his eyes half shut, though still remaining riveted to the serrated ridge far off. Instantly recognizing this trancelike state as that which he had exhibited on his former visit, I ceased speech and almost held my breath for fully a minute. It was Malvolio who broke the silence, murmuring in barely audible tones, "I wonder if we really could have turned that step on the way down."

I was enthralled. Was I really hearing these words from this most unlikely apparition, which had just now exhibited a total ignorance of and disinterest in mountaineering of a bygone age? I risked breaking the spell by quietly asking him what he meant. My venture worked—and his answer nearly made the flesh on the back of my neck crawl.

"Well, I say, we might have tried going out on the snow of the East Face. We might have negotiated a way around and got back onto the ridge a couple of hundred feet lower."

I was aghast. The English mode of speech, on top of the thrust of what he was saying, had me utterly spellbound, and an indefinable apprehension came over me. Who—or what—was I in the presence of? As calmly as I could control my stammering voice, I again ventured a question: "What did you do then?"

I was, I confess, almost relieved to note that this new interruption produced quite a different effect. Malvolio's head jerked around, his eyes torn from the distant ridge, his now-unclouded vision focused full on me, and he sullenly grunted, "What?"

"What did you do?" I repeated.

"I told you, I cleared the pipes, mister. If you're more careful about what goes down the toilet, you won't have these troubles. And it'd save me a long drive. I got to charge you for the time."

I waved him away, frustrated in my inquiries again. I was unable to think of any pretext for detaining him with any hope of reintroducing the trance-like effect that had produced such astounding words from such a pedestrian source.

But he was scarcely gone before my mind reeled with the enormity of this accidental and highly fortuitous discovery. I resolved to read up on mysticism, transcendentalism, reincarnation, and every form of the occult that I could lay my hands on. In scouring libraries over the next two weeks, I read more foolishness, charlatanism, and quackery than you could imagine and managed to uncover nothing remotely believable on the subject. A number of librarians gave me amused looks along with their assistance, and I soon began to feel quite foolish myself.

I don't recall at what point it suddenly occurred to me that the initials of Giovanni Malvolio were precisely those of George Mallory. Indeed, the first three letters of the last names were the same. I scarcely dared notice that Mr. Malvolio's apparent age could well put his birthdate somewhere around 1924—the year (perhaps the day?) of Mallory's disappearance and evident demise far away on the storm-swept upper slopes of Mount Everest.

With chilling determination, I knew I had to entice that strange dumpy figure of a man back out here. This time I would plan carefully how best to draw him out further, to try to maintain the trancelike state, to penetrate deeper into this inscrutable mystery.

A considerable portion of the next two days was spent in futile efforts to secure the cooperation of my bathroom pipes. Before the waters finally stopped. I had lost a couple of old Harvard banners, one T-shirt, and a purple-striped pajama top sent to me several Christmases ago by an obscure aunt. Where once those antebellum drains had been all too eager to clog up, they now swept all before them. Finally, though, that aunt's pajama top (well, not *her* pajama top, but you know what I mean) did the trick, and I was soon happily sloshing through water on the john floor toward the telephone to summon my hero of the sewers.

When the next day dawned, on which he had grumpily agreed to come for repairs, I was at first dismayed. A thick overcast of drizzly clouds totally obscured the view from my patio toward the cliffs and rock ridge that had touched off Mr. Malvolio's previous trancelike states and were the key to my present strategy. To my great relief, however, as the morning wore on, the weather improved just enough for visibility to extend to the cliff line; in fact, I nurtured the hope that the wild misty atmosphere that enshrouded the rocky heights might still further enhance the spirit in which those final days high on Everest might be recalled.

To the plumber's mind, my insistence on working outside on the patio on such a cold, damp morning may have confirmed his suspicion of my complete lunacy. However, he did get the pipes flowing again as before; and he did come to find me out on the patio as before.

For some reason, on this day his gaze did not come to rest on the distant cliffs as promptly as before. In fact, we went through a considerable exchange of forced dialogue, with me trying awkwardly to sustain the conversation while moving around in an effort to maneuver his line of vision to take the cliffs. I was beginning to feel quite foolish about the whole business, and would have let it drop in another minute. But then . . .

As before, Malvolio's eyes finally lit on the mountain horizon. His lids half closed; his voice trailed off, his jaw hanging slack in midphrase. He stood motionless, limp, transfixed.

With my nerves on end, I froze and waited an eternity for him to speak the first words. To my surprise and apprehension, something like a half smile slowly emerged on the plumber's normally inexpressive features. Then he said, "Exhilarating rock moves! Especially at that altitude. And then . . . clear sailing to the top!"

He paused. With a monumental effort to control my pounding heart, I spoke as quietly and calmly as I could. "Then you did make it to the summit?"

"Right to the top! No trouble at all on the upper snow slopes, except for being so deucedly exhausted from the thin air. 'Twas much easier coming down, that's certain."

I found myself numb and breathless. What had I stumbled onto? With infinite deliberation, I ventured the words, "Then, why did you fall?"

His reply came back in a stammer: "I . . . I thought . . . I thought I could find the route better if I went first. It didn't seem like difficult rock."

His eyes still riveted on the distant ridge, my companion continued, his voice even and calm: "It was Andy's problems down-climbing the rock. Of course, he'd have had no great difficulty if we'd been fresh. I assumed he could do the move, have no trouble with it."

As he spoke these words, I found myself drawn by the intensity of his gaze to look at the far-off ridge of rock above the precipitous cliff, with the wisps of old rainclouds still drifting around. As I looked out at this scene and heard the words spoken by Malvolio—or Mallory or whoever or whatever was speaking these strange, far-off words—I suddenly felt as if an unseen force racked my tense frame with one pervasive shock. Then I felt myself lapsing into a dreamlike state, my own eyes riveted on the distant rocks. The other voice came to me as through high, misty clouds:

"As he got to the hard move, I saw he was going to come off. I tried to get myself set to catch the fall when the rope came tight."

He paused. As if from afar, I heard my own voice say, "But if you had let me go down first, you might have held my fall from above. I knew I was going to fall in time to give you warning. You could have braced yourself, given me tension. We wouldn't both have fallen. You could have held us from above, instead of getting pulled off too. But you were in a hurry and insisted on going first."

He replied immediately: "But the moves were not hard."

"Not to you," I heard myself say. "But you knew I wasn't in your class as a rock climber. Particularly down-climbing. I'd never done much down-climbing in . . . "

My voice stopped as I felt the weight of his hand on my shoulder. "Andrew," he said, "what point are recriminations now? We fell—but we did not fail. We climbed it, didn't we? What could life have held for us after such a triumph? Where could we have gone on to from there?"

He may have said more, but my memory blanks out there. Apparently I blacked out, fell heavily on a wrought-iron bench, cutting my forehead, and stretched senseless on the patio. When I was next conscious, my neighbor was washing off the forehead cut, having somehow got me inside and placed me on a comfortable couch. When he saw that I was coming to, he asked how I was and, as I did not instantly reply, suggested that I might wish to get into drier clothes but otherwise take it easy till I felt better.

I half started up. "But where's Mallory?" I demanded.

"Who?" my neighbor looked somewhat puzzled, somewhat alarmed.

"Mal . . . Malvolio," I stammered. "The plumber."

"Oh yes, the fellow who called me over to look after you. He left fifteen minutes ago. Said the pipes ran fine now. Said he'd send you the bill."

My first instinct was to rush for my car, set off in wild pursuit. But a chilling fear overcame my curiosity. I would go after him later perhaps. Just at the moment I could recall little of our last words together, but the force of what we had discovered, groping together as we both gazed at the mist-shrouded rocky heights, gripped my thoughts.

At my neighbor's insistence I remained quiet; and, indeed, I found myself so physically and emotionally drained that I soon drifted into a profound sleep that carried me through the night.

When I awoke the next morning and was stumbling around trying to get myself breakfast, my neighbor reappeared, cheerfully inquiring how I felt this morning. I assured him I was OK, anxious not to remain subject to his protective scrutiny any longer than neighborly manners required. I was determined to set off to find Mr. Malvolio, wherever he was, whoever he was, to confront him with the enormity of our discovery.

With my thoughts thus occupied with these incredible concerns, it took me a while to realize what my neighbor was saying:

"Say, did you see that awful thing in this morning's paper. Little item in the second section. That plumber of yours, I think it was him. Malvolio—that was his name, wasn't it? His truck struck a bridge rampart on the interstate yesterday afternoon. On his way back from here, I suppose. He was killed instantly."

# STAIR-CASE TO STAR-LAND

## A STORY

by Laura Waterman

any young climbers are in Gary's position—devoured by such a desire to climb that all else in life is blotted out. In Gary's case, he is so new to the sport, so unfamiliar with the mores of cliff-side behavior, that he has not found the door that leads to partnerships with other climbers. Thrown on his own, Gary becomes a bewildered witness to disturbing events called up by idols he admires at the cliffs.

▲ ▼ ▲

**"Great, Gary! You cruised that overhang. You were smokin'," Phil says when Gary pulls** up onto the belay ledge. Phil hands his younger brother the gear sling, grinning. "Go for it, bro, the last pitch of the summer is your lead."

Gary's grinning too. But as he racks the nuts in order, smallest to largest, the way his brother has taught him, he keeps blinking. His eyes are smarting. Tomorrow Phil gets on that airplane for college and the summer's over. The summer Phil taught Gary to climb, and right now he wants it to last forever. Gary's glad Phil isn't saying anything. He doesn't trust his voice to answer.

Phil's staring straight ahead at the view of farmland and woodlots checkering the valley. The sun has sunk behind the cliff, filing the sky with translucent light. The backs of Phil's hands holding the rope are pitted and scabbed, one knuckle red and swollen.

Gary examines his own hands as he snaps carabiners onto the gear sling. The backs are like Phil's, just as scuffed by the rock, his fingertips just as callused.

"Buddy," Phil says, scrutinizing the sky as though he were decoding the future, "I'll be back at Thanksgiving. That's not so long. Now, get your ass up to the top. Hey, wait!" Phil's fingers tighten around his brother's forearm like vise grips. "Watch these guys. See? On *Billboard*? That's Carlo at the crux. It's one of his routes."

"Carlo. He's the one always climbing with Wells, right?"

"Wells, or more likely Sandi."

The brothers are silent studying Carlo, who's built like a linebacker, his curly black hair luminous in the fading light.

"Look at his shoulders. You wouldn't think a guy that size could climb," Phil says.

"But it's like he's weightless on the rock."

"I rubbed noses with *Billboard* once," Phil says. "My arms were spaghetti halfway up it. For me that route's two winters in the gym away."

They hear Carlo's crazy cackle as he sets up the belay.

"You can hear that guy all over the cliff," Phil says.

"Now his partner's starting up," Gary says.

"Yeah. Wells. The Professor."

"Why? Because he's skinny and wears glasses?"

"More than that. His whole approach to climbing, as if every pitch is the final exam."

"Boy, is he smooth," Gary whistles.

"Wells is graceful. But have you seen Sandi climb?" Phil says. "I've never seen anyone move up rock faster. She looks the way water would look if it could flow uphill. That blond hair blowing in the breeze. Yeah, Wells and Sandi. Everyone's favorite climbing couple. You know that route *Staircase to Starland*?

"That tops out on the flat slab at the highest point on the cliff?"

"That's the one. Exposed as hell and straight as spit. Wells and Sandi put that climb in together the day they became engaged. Their gift to each other, is what I heard." Phil's voice drifts off as he stares down to where Wells has joined Carlo at the belay. The ledge is just a few sketchy footholds, not sufficient room for both of them. "Anyway," Phil goes on, "when Wells and Sandi reached the top, they sat down at a tea carried over from the Mountain House. They'd do that for special occasions. I mean a proper English tea with scones and that thick Devonshire cream and raspberry jam. Or gooseberry or some quaint thing. Little cakes. Cucumber sandwiches with the crusts cut off. Get the picture? It was very sweet. These teas were a tradition. You can still find bits of broken crockery—sky blue cups with the Mountain House crest on them—in the dirt up there. Wells' and Sandi's was the last one."

"How come?"

"The benches and table on that flat slab finally got too shaky. You have to keep that rustic cedar stuff in repair or it all comes apart."

"But what a great place! Looking out over the best view in the world." Gary waves his arm toward the peaceful farmland valley.

"Romantic as hell," Phil grins. "Hey, get a move on, bro. If you want to get as good as those guys, you have to climb, climb, climb all the time. But," he chuckles, "you'll never be as good as Sandi, no matter if you climb every day for the rest of your life."

"And how am I going to climb at all with you off at college?" Gary asks. "I don't know any other climbers because I've climbed all summer with you." He reaches for a high handhold and starts up the last pitch, hating himself for sounding so ungrateful and whiny.

"Poor little brother. You're such a kid." Phil tilts back his head and yells up to him, "Just come up and hang around. Something's bound to happen."

▲ ▼ ▲

Gary rides his bike up to the cliff the next weekend. He walks along the old road—the carriage road everyone calls it—beneath the cliff, hands in pockets, gazing up at the climbers on hard routes. Climbers pass him in pairs, gear clanking. He doesn't have hardware or rope, so how can they know he's a climber too? All that stuff was Phil's.

He goes and hangs around the crowd working on boulder problems at the popular spot. At least you don't need gear for bouldering. A few times he works up the nerve to try a move, slotting his fingers in an overhanging crack and cranking up, aiming for the tiny footholds with the precision he admires in the best of the best. He visualizes himself swinging through moves with Carlo's strength or Wells' grace. But he knows he just looks awkward and stiff.

No one asks him to climb, though he forces himself to stay all day. He doesn't feel they're being *un*friendly; they just don't notice him. They arrive at the cliff in groups of two—already paired. Just as he had all summer with Phil. Still, he can't help feeling that if he looked better on the boulder problems, someone would ask him to climb.

He can't even bring himself to join in the banter. A couple of times he manages "Go for the heel hook" or "Crank it out, man," trying to sound like the other climbers who are casually joking around, waiting to take a turn on the boulder problems. But even to him these words sound forced. Once, as he lunges for a high handhold, he sings out, "Be there, baby!" but feels so ridiculous he falls off. He heard Carlo yell that once. It sounded so cool.

▲   ▼   ▲

The next Saturday Gary bikes in the dark up to the cliff, arriving at first light. There's only one car in the parking area, which will soon be overflowing with cars, and climbers sorting gear while gabbing about hard routes and close calls. He knows he'll have the cliff to himself, just the way he has planned it.

He decides on an easy climb—the first one Phil took him on—and starts up. He doesn't really want to be soloing. He knows it's dangerous. You have to know what you're doing to climb rock without a rope. The rock is cold. His fingers go stiff, and after a few moves he can't feel the in-cut holds. His legs are shaking, his mouth is dry, and he can hear himself panting as though he's fighting for oxygen at twenty-eight thousand feet. But he keeps going because if he pauses to warm his hands he'll lose momentum. And probably his resolve. If he backs down now he knows he'll never get up the nerve to come back. He's climbing like a beginner, clutching at the rock, jerking his way up this pitch, but it's weird without a rope, without Phil.

113

Gary claws onto the broad belay ledge halfway up the cliff and sprawls on the gravel, his heart banging in his ears. His shirt is clammy under his sweater and he wipes his sweaty palms on his pants, leaving dirt smears. The muscles in his forearms bulge, aching from hauling himself up this easy pitch. "Shit," he mumbles. "I was out of control." He turns and sits with his back to the rock, hugging his knees, and the sunrise hits him in the face. He watches it burn off the fog, revealing the familiar valley of cornfields, pastures, woods. *Wow! I wish Phil could see this.*

He hears something to his left and looks across the cliff face. Wells is climbing solo, too. So that explains the lone car in the parking lot.

Gary sits very still, not wanting to disturb Wells's concentration. The way Wells moves—deliberate, selecting the best holds in a steady rhythmic way—Gary's sure he's on a hard climb. Wells is smooth, like an athlete taking the hurdles stride after well-timed stride. *That's how to do it, dummy.* Gary watches as Wells leans out on his handholds, poised like a hawk on an updraft, and takes a hand off the rock, then shoves up his glasses. The Professor! Gary slides back into a shadowed corner as Wells glides on by. Wells so obviously knows what he's doing that Gary feels like an impostor.

But Gary promises himself that's going to change. And after a few weekends of biking up to the cliff at dawn, Gary begins to feel like a solo climber, too. At least until his brother returns. Wells is always on the cliff, so it's him and Wells doing this dawn solo-climbing together. Though Wells is always on extreme routes and has never—not once—glanced in Gary's direction.

And what's happened to Sandi? Does she sleep in or what?

▲   ▼   ▲

Gary is halfway up the cliff and feeling something's missing, not a conscious thought, just aware that the morning's out of order. Where's Wells? It hits Gary how much safer he feels with Wells in view on a nearby climb. He scans the cliff, hoping to spot Wells, and instead sees Carlo's curly black hair. He's climbing with Sandi. Looks like they're on *Collision Course,* and since Gary wants Phil to take him on this hard climb when he's back for Thanksgiving, when Gary gains the belay ledge he sits down to watch.

Sandi is leading. She's a bright bit of red fleece jacket and wild blond hair. Flowing up the pitch faster than would seem possible, just as Phil had said.

Quiet, too. No rattling of gear against the rock. She gains the ledge and has Carlo on belay in seconds. No words exchanged. Gary likes how silent they are; he feels it as respect for the stillness of the dawn. Carlo powers up to the ledge. Broad shoulders in lime green sitting very close to Sandi. They hold that pose, gazing off into the rising sun flooding the valley with morning light.

Gary wishes they'd get on with it. His muscles are cooling down now. *Come on, you guys. I have to get moving.* He stands up, about to forget it, when Carlo and Sandi turn toward each other and kiss. At least Gary thinks that's what's happening. Carlo is holding Sandi's face between his hands, but they're a good 150 feet below him.

Yeah. They are. They're deep into it. Black hair and blond. Lime green on red, as Carlo eases Sandi backward, onto the belay ledge. Shit. He wishes he weren't seeing this. Where's Wells? It's supposed to be Sandi and Wells, everyone's favorite climbing couple, Phil had told him. *Staircase to Starland.*

Gary starts up the rock. He has to get out of here or else he'll see the rest of it. But, Christ, this pitch is harder than he thought. He breaks into a sweat, his fingers slipping, feeling freaked by easy moves turned tough.

▲ ▼ ▲

The next Saturday he's back on the rock, hoping not to see anything like what he saw last time.

Gary picks a climb near the highest part of the cliff and concentrates on focused movement, like Wells. He savors the rough quartzite with its in-cut holds that fit his fingers. He feels strong. He feels an inner lightness that makes him want to shout. Phil will be home in a month! Gary can't wait to show his brother how *good* he is now.

Sitting on the belay ledge, taking in this peaceful valley view of farms, he could convince himself he made the whole thing up between Carlo and Sandi. He leans back against the hard rock. The sun is about to break.

His ears prick. It's coming from above. Rockfall. No, like birds taking off. Rock doves that nest under overhangs. They're cackling. No. Not birds. It's Carlo's zany laugh. What's he doing at the top of the cliff? Gary cranes his neck up in time to see Carlo launch a running dive into thin air.

Arms spread wide like a bird's wings, curly black head thrown back. *He's twenty-five feet out. No rope. Bloody Christ, he's going to hit the carriage road.* Gary leans instinctively forward, his body tense, following Carlo's downward trajectory. Hears the bone-cracking smack, like hitting concrete from three hundred feet off the deck. Gary winces as he watches Carlo's body bounce once on the talus boulders, then lie still, his limbs splayed at funny angles, like a long-legged insect smashed on a car windshield.

Gary breaks into a sweat. He doesn't dare move because he's shaking so bad. His stomach lurches and he starts to retch.

After a while, when the sun begins to warm the rocks, some climbers spot Carlo's body—a lime green smudge—on the talus below the cliff face. "Carlo! Oh, God, it's Carlo!" Their voices carry up to Gary. He watches as more and more come pounding down the carriage road, gear clanking. They litter the body off the boulders, passing the stretcher from hand to hand. Then they march along the carriage road, at least a hundred climbers, silent now, like a cortége, bearing Carlo's broken body. Gary keeps looking for Wells, or Sandi. They're not there.

Finally, he stops shaking enough to climb to the top, runs down the trail, and mounts his bike. Races down the carriage road at reckless speed, knowing he can't brake fast enough if he meets a walker rounding a curve. He chucks the bike and works out on boulder problems in the woods until he's worn the skin off his callused fingers. The sun has set and the light's bad, but he pushes it until he misses a high hold and crashes onto a jutting rock, gouging his shin.

He can feel blood oozing down his leg as he pedals painfully back along the carriage road. Very little light is left and everyone has gone.

As he passes below the start of *Staircase to Starland* he looks up. There's Wells, crouched down among the blocky boulders where Carlo landed.

Gary hobbles up the slope. Wells doesn't look up. He's staring at some leaves he's holding in his hands. "Carlo's life's blood," he says in a throaty voice, and lets the leaves drop through his fingers. Gary sees they're smeared with rust-colored splotches.

"Jesus. Look what you did to your leg," Wells says, looking at Gary. His eyes behind his glasses are such an intense shade of blue he looks a little mad.

"Yeah," Gary says.

"That's a bloody mess." Wells picks up some fragments of pottery from the dirt and stands up. "Come on," he says and starts down the talus slope.

"Where are we going?" Gary asks.

"To the hospital. You need stitches."

▲ ▼ ▲

In the van Wells says, "Here, wrap this around that gash." He reaches be-hind his seat, steering with one hand, and pulls out a towel. "It's not very clean, but they'll pump you full of antibiotics. I don't want you dripping on my upholstery. There's been enough blood let loose around here for one day." He lashes a look at Gary. "You saw him jump, kid?"

Gary nods. "He looked so great."

"What's that supposed to mean, huh?"

"In the air. He was soaring. It was perfect."

"You think. Well, he botched it." Wells wipes his hand across his mouth. "What?"

"My friend Carlo *meant* to crash-land on the carriage road. That's what his fucking note said: splatter his guts all over the carriage road." Wells fixes Gary with those cobalt eyes, which his glasses only magnify. "Well, he missed. Not even close. Came bashing down through that goddamn tree."

"Uh," Gary says.

"His note, by the way, was addressed to Sandi. You probably know that Sandi's my wife."

"Uh," Gary says.

"Can't you say anything other than 'uh'?" Wells pushes up his steel frames with a forefinger. "Tell me what you saw. The details."

Gary moves in his seat. His leg is throbbing now. "I don't know. I was on that easy climb next to *Staircase.* I heard cackling, you know, like rock doves. It made me look up and he streaks over the top. Over my head. I saw he didn't have a rope. I was scared. But he looked so great. I mean, he was *flying,*" Gary says. He wraps his arms around his chest. He's starting to shake the way he did on the ledge. "That cackling, that was him."

"I'm sure Carlo would be glad someone admired his exit."

"*Staircase to Starland.* That was your climb, wasn't it?"

"And Sandi's." Wells pulls the broken crockery out of his pocket and passes the chips to Gary. "Look," he says.

The shards are an intense dark blue, like the sky in winter. Gary turns them over in his hands. One has a picture of the Mountain House on it.

"The engagement tea," he whispers, staring at the broken bits.

"You got it. His note said, 'taking your precious teacups for the ultimate ride.' "

"You mean . . . ?"

"That my buddy Carlo jumped with these very pieces in his outstretched hands."

The van hurtles on through the darkness. Gary glances at the speedometer, which is hovering between eighty and eighty-five.

"It was a great climb," Gary says. "I was hoping to climb it when I got good enough."

"We liked the direct line. Sandi said she saw it as the path of our married life together: from this day forth till death—that kind of crap," Wells says and takes a curve at a leaping speed, throwing Gary against the door. "You probably know that soloing can be bad for your health."

Gary shrugs and looks at Wells.

"Yeah. I solo. But I'm a better climber than you. You've got to have your shit together. Guys get hurt bad who don't."

"But I saw you on the hardest routes."

"It was the only way I could handle things at the time. Know what I mean?"

"But I thought you said—"

"That's *how* I kept *my* shit together." Wells pulls out, passing on a curve. "You just started climbing, right? What's your name, anyway?"

"Gary. I climbed with my brother this summer. He taught me."

"So, where's your brother, Gary?"

"College. Away."

"And you don't know anyone else to climb with? Barge on in and *ask*, for chrissake. You're bold on the rock."

"I didn't know you'd ever seen . . . how did you know I saw Carlo jump?"

"I see everything. Or thought I did." The speedometer zooms up toward ninety.

They are silent a few minutes. Wells eases up on the gas pedal. He takes the exit for the hospital and pulls into the emergency-room parking lot. He turns off the motor, but his hands still squeeze the wheel. The light from the high poles bounces off his wire-rims, scarring his face with zigzag lines.

"Look at that towel. You've soaked it, for godsakes," Wells says, then laughs, a choked sound.

"I hope I'll be all right by Thanksgiving when my brother comes back." Gary casts a look at his leg.

"You'll be fine. I'll see you up there in the dawn hours way before then. We can do a climb." Wells slumps in his seat. "If I ever go climbing again."

"You'll climb," Gary says, swiveling to face Wells. "You'll climb. Same as me. You can't stop. Not now."

# A TROUBLED TALE OF THE NOTCH OF THE MOUNTAINS

## A STORY

by Guy Waterman

**W**hen working on one of our climbing histories, we were obliged to read innumerable handwritten manuscripts of interminable length and irretrievable handwriting, because they conveyed vital information on early ascents. Saturated with that ornate prose of the 1820s, Guy was inspired to fight back with a parody of the style. Many of the facts mentioned were indeed historical. The Notch of the Mountains was the name most often used in the early days for what was later named Crawford Notch, as it is styled today. Ethan Crawford was an innkeeper there during the 1820s. The Willey family, homesteaders in the heart of the Notch, perished in a landslide in 1826. At any rate, we sent this off to the editor of *Appalachia,* Sandy Stott, with a note saying that a (mythical) friend named Winslow Thratchett had sent the manuscript to us. We said we had no idea who the author was, or the date, but presumed it was written shortly after the famous landslide, possibly in 1827. First, Sandy wrote back saying it was much too long. So, after a couple of weeks, we wrote back, saying, Guess what! Thratchett found another copy of the 1827 manuscript, and this one was much shorter! To his great credit, Sandy published it with a perfectly straight face, using the following contributor's note:

This manuscript, apparently written by a Mr. Sheldrake (first name unknown) in or shortly after 1827, was discovered by Winslow Thratchett, White Mountains history buff. It was made available to *Appalachia* through the courtesy of Laura and Guy Waterman, frequent contributors to this journal.

We have no idea what proportion of *Appalachia*'s readers detected the spoof. Parody, yes, but we did try to sneak in a message.

**Source:** December 15, 1996, issue of *Appalachia*.

▲ ▼ ▲

**The faint gleam from the window of Ethan Allen Crawford's mountain inn finally** penetrated the dripping gloom of the rain-drenched forest. Greatly relieved was I to see that warm light, as but an hour of dwindling twilight remained for me to find my weary way through the depressing wilderness. I had survived the most harrowing night of what I had previously regarded as a reasonably adventurous life.

Often had I traveled in the harsh north woods of New Hampshire and Vermont, my associations with the fur trade taking me there from my home in the cultivated port of Portland, Maine. No stranger was I to these hostile White Mountains, nor to the gloomy Notch of the Mountains through which I had to pass between Portland and the north country.

Yet I had never before found myself benighted in that dread rocky defile, enclosed on all sides by hideous precipice, no light for comfort, and haunted by events of a most uncommon twist, as I shall relate in this narrative.

▲ ▼ ▲

This was the summer of 1827, and the Notch of the Mountains was still ravaged by the effects of that terrible storm and landslide of the previous summer, which had buried the family of Samuel Willey at their homestead in the heart of the Notch. The entire family perished: only a solitary dog was left alive, half-crazed, haunting the spectral scene, fearful and unapproachable in its distress, almost a symbol of that wild untamed hostile mountainscape. As reminders of that horrid storm, uprooted trees still lay across the path, to which new devastation was being added by the all-day rains and high winds of this day in 1827 when I plied my way north along the solitary track.

At first I struggled through this chaotic scene with reasonable dispatch, and passed the site of the Willey tragedy not long after noon, with confidence of completing my journey in daylight. But a few steps farther, I found my way blocked by a sizable fallen pine, one that evidently had crashed to earth within a few hours. It cost me no little time and exertion to circumvent this obstacle. When I regained the trail, considerably wetter for my struggles through branches and undergrowth, I found to my chagrin that the swollen stream had carried away a section of bank on which the trail had formerly been lodged. It was needful to plunge anew into thickets of lush spring growth, heavy with rain and hiding uncertain footing beneath. On the downhill side, the swift and deep waters of the stream raced below; on the uphill side, the steepening banks of the mountain made progress difficult. After fifty feet or so of this struggle, I regained the trail. But it had now taken me perhaps an hour to move scarcely a stone's throw from the Willey House.

Around the next bend of the path I was further dismayed to find that a slender log bridge, hastily erected the previous fall to replace one washed away in last August's storm, was so far threatened by the rising flood as to be already under an inch or two of water. Although the water-washed logs made slippery footing, I crossed safely—but as I took the last step, my added weight proved too much for what was left of the upper bank's supporting earth. I looked back with consternation to see the bridge swept away down the swollen stream.

Now feeling the first signs of apprehension for what yet remained of my passage through the Notch, and realizing with trepidation that retreat was no longer possible, I moved ahead somewhat more in haste. Repeatedly, downed trees and washed sections of the trail compelled me to plunge back into the water-soaked undergrowth. My most energetic efforts, accordingly, failed to carry me higher in the Notch as fast as I had to go if I were to reach the rock gateway in the fading light.

As I pushed through branches around the bend of the trail, yet another fallen tree blocked my path—and here I came upon a sight so pathetic that it altered my frame of mind considerably, leaving me to undergo the rest of my adventure in a still more distressed state. Directly beneath the gigantic trunk lay the crushed body of what I at first took for a large fox, but which proved upon inspection to be a dog. The unfortunate victim was a rich golden brown in color, some north woods family's beloved house pet, I conjectured. A grotesque detail I noted was that one ear had been sheared off completely—by a crashing branch, I assumed—leaving the handsome head with a strange, almost comical look. The accident must have just occurred, the body being still warm. It saddened me to think of some beloved family pet wandering so far afield, to be struck down so cruelly. The nearest habitation would have to be below Abel Crawford's or above Ethan's, six miles in either direction. What had possessed so lovely a creature, so out of place in this dismal Notch, to come so far on such a day—to meet so grim a destiny?

Hastily leaving this unhappy scene, I worked my way around this latest obstacle, becoming more depressed by the circumstances in which I found myself. At length, after an especially large blowdown had forced me to clamber over boulders and branches for a considerable distance, I found to my great discomfort that I could not locate the trail on the far side. In the gathering gloom I cast about in several directions, but soon found myself so disoriented as to be unable to regain the ruined pathway where I had been but minutes before. And so it was that I resolved reluctantly to seek some natural shelter of tree or rock under which to endure the night, trusting to morning light and a wished abatement of the storm to enable me to find my way either up or down out of the Notch, with or without the ruined trail.

▲ ▼ ▲

I was not as fearful as many might be at the prospect of a dark and rainy night out in these savage woods. I am possessed of a calm and rational temperament, which stands me well in such straits. Besides, I have always carried a loaded pistol in travels through wilderness country, as precaution against bear or the occasional panther. Other than these, no savage creatures remain to surprise the traveler in these enlightened years. Wolves have been gone from these parts for years, though idle rumors can be heard. But with my calm and rational temperament, I did not think twice about wolves as I settled myself for the long night.

And so, in that rocky, boulder-strewn defile, I calmly found a projecting arm of rock large enough to afford shelter from the never-ceasing rain, with headroom to allow standing awkwardly in one place, or sitting upon a large tree root sufficiently comfortable to permit some hours of sleep.

In the dead of this evil night, I awoke with a sudden apprehension at the sound, clearly distinguished even in the tumult of a storm, of padding footsteps in the undergrowth outside. Straining to see through the dark, I slowly grew aware of a shadowy silhouette against the dark night sky: an outline of a large animal's head, one ear cocked in my direction. For one moment it seemed to my alarmed spirit that the head I regarded was that of a dog—a one-eared dog at that. But I dismissed that wild notion and realized that either I faced a bear or indeed wolves had not entirely quit these forests; not this one, at least.

In either event, immediate use of my firearm was called for. With as calm but rapid a motion as I could muster, I produced my pistol and fired at the menacing silhouette. I heard the thump of a falling body in the bushes, and the vision was gone from the night sky.

You may well imagine that I slept but little for the rest of that miserable night. Rainfall continuing until dawn, together with my ignorance of which way to proceed, prevented any thought of moving during the night. Even had my tree root been as comfortable as Eve's bower, my consciousness of the dread beast's body just a few feet away kept my nerves on ragged edge throughout the awful hours of darkness, until at long last approaching morning lightened considerably the gloom.

Filled with morbid anxiety, I roused myself to go look upon the spot where the spectral silhouette had appeared before me during the night. There I beheld—nothing! No bear, no wolf—indeed, no track in the underbrush or mud. Nothing! Puzzled, and beset with vague foreboding of the most uncomfortable sort, at first I had difficulty in turning full attention to the more pressing requirement of my own survival: to find the trail, to the extent it still existed, and gain the gateway of the Notch.

The remaining struggles of that day live in my mind as a prolonged nightmare: clambering over boulders and tree trunks, fighting soaking branches and bushes, weakened by my lack of food and sleep, finding and losing again and again the ruined track, struggling against inward fears as well as outward dangers. By midafternoon, however, I at last struggled up the steep and narrow incline through the gateway of the Notch. I had escaped that tangled wild labyrinth!

As I threw myself upon a rock for rest, my perils over, my heart suddenly chilled to hear a long-drawn howl pierce the air. So wolves were indeed still in the Notch, thought I! I listened in vain for a repetition of the eerie wail, but there was none.

In normal travel, it is but an hour and a half's stroll from the head of the Notch to the younger Crawford's hospitable door. In my weakened and demoralized state, and with resumption of a steady rain, the journey took me until nightfall, so that the first sight of Ethan Crawford's light came as immense relief to my mounting anxiety that I might face another night out, perhaps more rain, perhaps another bear or wolf—I knew not what, but imagined altogether too much.

▲ ▼ ▲

Dried and refreshed by the warmth of Mr. Crawford's hearth and table, I was encouraged to relate my misadventures in struggling through the chaotic Notch. Both Mr. Crawford and the small group of travelers sharing his accommodations were attentive, especially when I described my nighttime encounter with the beast.

But when I went on to the sad incident with the dog pinned beneath the tree, I thought I noticed a subtle change in the calm good cheer of my host. When I described his golden fur, Mr. Crawford grew quiet and stared at the fire, and I observed that one of his servants, a sullen old wretch named Raithby, left his seat in the corner to creep unobtrusively nearer our little circle. The other guests showed sympathy for the unfortunate pet's fate, but, to my disappointment, Mr. Crawford suddenly rose and announced that one who had endured such perils and hardships as I must surely need rest, and directed Raithby to light me to my room.

Raithby conducted me silently upstairs, but, once in the room, he whirled and glared at me over the candle, his old wrinkled face tensed, and demanded in an urgent whisper, "Beggin' your pardon, Mr. Sheldrake, sir, but did ye notice anythin' peculiar about that dog's ears?"

"Not ears," I replied, determined not to show unease over the surly fellow's demeanor. "Ear. The poor brute had but one, the other apparently—"

"Ye thought 'im dead," hissed the insolent old servant, his face screwed up to mirror the distorted otherworldly import of his words. "You, sir, saw the dog who belonged to the house of Samuel Willey, sir. Did until last summer. That dog with the one ear showed up in Bartlett two days after the slide, come 'round to the Lovejoy farm, Mrs. Willey's people. One of Mrs. Willey's brothers, Josh Lovejoy, he said the brute must have gone mad, the wild savage creature. So he took a shotgun and dropped 'im with a single shot, right there at the edge of the woods. But when they went to look for the body, they couldn't find nothin'. Nothin' there at all!

"Just one week later, a crew from Abel Crawford's was rebuildin' a bridge farther down. Someone looked up and, by God, there was this dog with the golden coat and just one ear, runnin' down the road toward them. When it got close, it turned off into the woods and they saw no more trace—but they knowed they'd seen 'im on the road.

"Last winter, down at the Lovejoy place, they heard low moanin' durin' the night out near the woodshed. They went out but couldn't find nothin' in the dark—but in the mornin' there was dog tracks all aroun'.

"Worst of all was the howls. Oh, those howls! We been hearin' these ghostly howls toward nightfall comin' from the heart of the Notch. Here we be, laborin' all our lives to bring civilization to this wilderness, and this godforsaken creature comes sneakin' around the edges of our lives, howlin' to remind us of a past we're tryin' to forget.

"Some say the wolves are back in the Notch—but we knows different, sir. An' when you say you saw that crazy, driven beast pinned under a tree during the storm, I tell you, sir, it'll take more than one tree to set down that dog for good—if mortal dog indeed he be, and not some mad infernal specter of wildness sent to haunt the Notch of the Mountains till we an' all our civilization be gone ourselves."

At length Raithby paused. Tired as I was, his tale had held me as tightly as his grip upon my wrist, which I now disengaged, and with a strong effort to recover my normal calm and rational temperament, I said, "Mr. Raithby, you have discharged your duty of showing me to my accommodations as Mr. Crawford directed. Further, your ghost story has been entertaining and original. I've never heard one in which a common household pet has replaced the usual white-sheeted figures. But now, if you will excuse yourself, I have had two long days of—"

The sullen old fellow interrupted again: "Ghost story, ye say? Beggin' your pardon, sir, but that 'bear' ye shot: Did ye get a good look? Did ye see anything unusual about 'im?"

My mind flickered back to that ghostly scene—but I declined to be drawn into this nonsense further and this time succeeded in getting the surly fool to leave. Yet, even after two days of active exertions without good rest, I found myself tormented by Mr. Crawford's aged menial. At last, however, blessed sleep came. At breakfast I avoided the gloomy stare of old Raithby, but did resolve to seek opportunity to question my good host on the curious and unexplained circumstances that troubled my thoughts.

In my distraught and exhausted condition, I had elected to rest all that day at the inn, but with other company present no private occasion arose between me and Mr. Crawford. On the following morning, the weather now entirely clear, all other guests moved on their various ways, so that by midday my good host and I were left alone in the comfortable common room, and I opened the subject that concerned me.

"Mr. Crawford, you were, I believe, among the first at the scene of the unfortunate Willeys' disaster?"

"Ah, yes, Mr. Sheldrake," said my host, a great sadness crossing his benign features. "It was indeed my sorrowful duty to help determine the awful fate of the family."

I expressed sympathy for their plight and the task of the rescuers, then continued. "Was there any living creature that survived that terrible landslide?"

"No, sir," replied the good man, "not one human soul but perished in that terrific manifestation of the Almight—"

I interrupted: "No human souls; but besides the human, Mr. Crawford? Were there any living creatures left?"

I fancied my host's relaxed features clouded as he responded, "Living creatures, Mr. Sheldrake? Ah, yes, I do recall in the stables were two oxen. One was actually pinned under fallen timbers, so near—"

"But besides oxen," I pressed, "was there no other living creature? A dog perhaps?"

Ethan Crawford rose from his chair and began to pace up and down. "Mr. Sheldrake, there are strange tales told about the Willeys' pet dog. He did survive the landslide and has shown remarkable facility for other narrow escapes. But I urge you to give no moment's consideration to silly supernatural interpretations put upon certain incidents by local gossip. I give firm assurance that, case by case, perfectly calm and rational explanations are evident.

"Some of the tale-tellers make much of this dog's strong attachment to little Jerry Willey, the eleven-year-old whose body has yet to be found. Rumor has arisen that the forsaken animal will roam the Notch, survive any doom, aye, and howl and scare every traveler that passes through my humble doors, until the day that poor little Jerry Willey's remains finally are laid to rest in a proper grave."

My host fell silent for some moments, and when he resumed he looked me full in the face. "Mr. Sheldrake, some of us came here and found a wild country. And we have devoted ourselves, body and spirit, to taming the country, exorcising wildness, and establishing a modest civilization in these rugged hills. We neither welcome nor credit the specter of a past we seek to stamp out."

The conversation continued for some minutes, but my host soon steered to other topics that I do not recall. Presently I called for my reckoning, thanked my good host, avoided the glance of the miserable Raithby, and prepared to resume my journey under clear skies and in a northerly direction, away from the sinister scenes that had brought me such anguish during the storm.

Just as I lifted the latch to leave, however, a swarm of young workmen rushed across the threshold and jostled into Mr. Crawford's inn, wild-eyed and jabbering confusedly. The only figure I recognized was that of young Josh Lovejoy, the unfortunate Mrs. Willey's brother. Mr. Crawford commanded the group to retire to the kitchen, but I drew one of their number aside and learned from him the reason for their astonishing commotion.

My informant related that these workmen had been at labor in the very heart of the Notch through which I had passed two days before, digging foundations for a new bridge below the old Willey house. There the men had made a grisly discovery: the remains of a child's body, so far deteriorated as to be little more than a skeleton. Considerable discussion ensued as to whether these bones might constitute the final remains of one of the Willey children when Joshua Lovejoy suddenly cried a terrible oath and dashed up the bank to fetch his gun. The others first thought the poor man overwrought by the discovery of one of his little nephews; this impression strengthened when Joshua began to cry out "infernal beast," "that godforsaken monster," and "Satan's own cur." Then, however, all saw it: a great golden-haired dog, standing motionless on the farther bank, gazing intently at the unearthed remains of the child, nose quivering with excitement, his one ear cocked forward eagerly. With one shot from Joshua's gun, the animal slumped forward and was still.

Like a madman, Joshua leaped into the stream, yelling to the skies that the brute's body must be seized and forever entombed in the earth that had covered him many times before. He carried the carcass back across the stream, heedless alike of the swift current and the stench of the dead animal. They buried the child's bones—now convinced that they must be those of little Jerry Willey—with the carcass of his beloved dog. Both lay now under several feet of earth and rocks, interred for eternity in the silent gloom of the Notch of the Mountains.

As my informant concluded his chilling tale, Mr. Crawford appeared and dispatched him to the kitchen as well. Left again to ourselves, we stepped outside to behold below us to the south the lofty mountainscape through which cut the Notch, late the scene of such disquieting events. My host seemed anxious to assure me that I need fear no further frights from the superstitions and rumors to which such as old Raithby and workmen were susceptible. I thanked him for his solicitude and commended his calm and rational approach to these matters. We then mused some moments on the exceptional chronicle of the fate of the Willey family, from that terrible storm of the previous August to this final resting of the surviving animal and his beloved but ill-starred human companion. We both perceived the outcome as forever closing a chapter in the wild character of this north country. The specter of savage wildness was now laid to rest; the gentler, more refined influences of civilized life could now proceed unhaunted by primitive fears and brute superstitions.

Just before I turned to resume my northern journey, the two of us gazed a moment southward toward the spot where the wild mist-shrouded mountainsides closed in to form the great Notch four miles below. Suddenly, in the still of that summer's day, a faint but unmistakable sound reached our ears. It was a long-drawn rising howl, ascending from the dark depths of the Notch, a muffled but impervious crescendo, not loud yet penetrating, oppressing all refined sensibility with a foreboding. It seemed a voice that would not die, maychance shall never die.

I stared at my host, incredulous. Mr. Crawford seemed to grow pale and shudder, then summon a great effort to relax his features. He said to me in his kindliest tones, "Well, Mr. Sheldrake, perhaps there is after all a wolf or two still roaming these mountains. You do hear stories, and certainly that was a wolf's howl, was it not? But just one or two in these great woods surely constitute no risk to human civilization, do they?"

Without offering opportunity for my reply, he bade farewell and strode back into the warm solace of his comfortable inn.

# CLIMBING WITH MARGARET

## A STORY

by Laura Waterman

**A**fter I had finished this story, I realized I had written it because I had lost my own climbing life. Too many years of pounding descents had at last squeezed the spring out of my knees and rung down the final curtain on my ability to enjoy descending from climbs. So I stopped climbing and started writing short stories. This tale of recollection captured through fiction is for countless climbs shared with Guy, but also, in a special way, for the last climbs I shared with my friend Sue. (Unlike Margaret, Sue is alive and well.)

**Source:** "Climbing with Margaret" first appeared in *Solo: On Her Own Adventure*, edited by Susan Fox Rogers (Seattle: Seal Press, 1996). It was reprinted in *Gifts of the Wild: A Woman's Book of Adventures,* from the editors of Adventura Books (Seattle: Seal Press, 1998).

▲ ▼ ▲

**She stopped moving upward. Time spun itself out so that tasks she knew took only a** second, such as placing an ice ax, took hours. Stalled, she leaned out on her tools and looked up at the sky, dark and scabbed with hard stars. Her eyes moved to the soft void on her right, blank and without sound.

She let her arms hang out in her wrist loops, dropped her head forward to touch the ice. She wasn't using the rope, but it was in her pack. Her head repeated: *partners belay partners belay partners* with such tedium it made her gag.

A voice! It nearly tipped her backward and she felt wild from the adrenaline as she caught herself. Where am I? That voice sounded so high and weak. It made her laugh! She rested her head again on the raw flank of the mountain until her brow went numb. She made herself kick in her left crampon, and the ice cracked like brittle bone. "Damn you, Margaret," she said.

She had arrived in Talkeetna first, as they had planned, and began re-packing the food. She expected Margaret in two days. But she wasn't on the passenger van that arrived from Anchorage. She called the university where Margaret taught and someone with a voice like crushed ice told her, "Didn't you hear? Professor Simon was in an accident last night on her way to the airport. A tractor-trailer jumped the median. It took out several cars."

No, she hadn't heard. Was she . . . ? "Not dead," the voice said. "Professor Simon is in a coma. Her spine is broken. They fear brain damage."

She returned to the building where she had left their gear and walked around, touching things, bending to pick up fragments of herself. Ropes, snow pickets, carabiners, ice screws, webbing, rock gear, the stove, pots, fuel, their tent, their sleeping bags—ready for climbing. Her eyes felt parched.

She had had herself flown in anyway. After all, it was to be their fiftieth-birthday climb.

▲ ▼ ▲

Time slid back to normal and she continued climbing. After a while she knew Margaret had reached the alcove and was waiting there. Or perhaps she wouldn't wait, but would keep just ahead, hedged behind the dark. She heard the soft *thunk, thunk* of Margaret's tools, and imagined Margaret's hands gripping the shafts, relaxed in the wrist loops. She felt the power of Margaret's surging swing vibrate down her own arm.

The alcove: where the avalanche caught them last time. Not a direct hit, just a sideswipe when the snow slope slid. She was belaying under a skimpy rock overhang and had a gallery seat when a Niagara-like rush of snow and ice spewed in front of her nose and out onto the glacier, creating a mound the size of a New England hill. "Margaret! Margaret!" "Fay! Fay!" Their cries rang in the turbulent air dense with snow dust. She had fully expected the rope to go slack and was surprised not to see Margaret whirl by, a cartwheel of arms and legs and ice chunks. "Heck, Fay, it missed me by fifty feet, easy. Just noisy, that's all. I was more concerned about you. It was big!"

The avalanche creamed their route, removing all their anchors and fixed ropes, which they discovered when they began rappelling. Not an ice screw remained. They were two-thirds of the way up the mountain.

They had lost too much to improvise with scanty gear, and after that they had to admit they were too undone to go on.

Her eye caught the headlight of a star skidding toward her, and she clenched her tools, in a panic over being nudged into nothingness. She saw the tractor-trailer, lit up for night travel, blasting the median. She clawed to her left, crampons screeching. Her tongue turned to sawdust in her mouth, and she smelled her own bitter sweat. Cars were upturned, scattered like jackstraws. The New England hill hardened into a concrete burial mound.

▲ ▼ ▲

"The Alaska Range is not for sissies. That's what some climber told me, Fay, after my slide show. Oh God!" Margaret laughed. "The Alaska Range makes me go weak in the knees faster than I can sink an ice screw."

They had hooted their way up a whole summer of routes with this line. Mouths caked dry down into their throats. Hands sweating inside gloves, feet freezing in damp socks, minds riding high on animal instinct. How they both loved it. How she still loved it.

The stars dimmed. She paused and pushed her cuff back to check the time. The liver spots on the back of her hand glowed faint as phosphorus.

She looked up. It was light enough now to see the outline of the overhang. Her heart caught. Its form had lived in her nighttime thoughts for so long. The way the rock tunneled into the snow slope, making a cavelike space tall enough to stand in if you were short, then sloping to a crawlspace at the back. Exactly the same.

She scrambled up, her crampons biting into the firm snow under the overhang. She had stood right here to belay Margaret. The crack she'd slotted a chock into was—she fell to her knees and crawled to the back of the

133

alcove, reached to rub rime off the rock—here. She tore off her glove and ran her bare fingers into the rough crack. It had been five years.

"But I can stop right here," she said aloud, on her knees before the crack. The rock dug into her fingers. Margaret was ahead, on the upper snow slopes. It was getting light now.

▲ ▼ ▲

"After all, Fay," she heard Margaret's voice, "we're perfect. You teach writing, all that woolgathering and horsing around of imagination, and I keep us solid with math and logic."

She, Fay, was an Easterner; precisely, a New Englander who taught in a college town of white clapboard buildings set on a village green. Joe taught there too. Fay arranged her classes in order to be home when her children came home. She could be counted on to make pies for church suppers. But she could see that the folks she ran into at the post office felt uncomfortable with her peeling nose and raw brow. *Rash* was the word she picked up on the supermarket line. It made her smile at her weather-browned hands.

Margaret had spent four years in a New England college, which was where they had met and first climbed together. Then she had returned to Berkeley.

"You're more rooted than I am," Fay told Margaret, "and if we didn't climb together every summer that would be the end of us." She watched Margaret's hands in the Cascades, the Alps, and once in the Andes, one holding the pot steady, the other stirring the dinner, the skin taut and fine-lined as an etching. Hairline thin, white scars.

The two of them had gone climbing even when her children were small, even when Joe said two weeks was his limit. Then he changed his mind. "We love canned spaghetti, Fay. Take three."

Margaret never had kids. She hardly had a husband. "Oh, Richard?" Fay heard impatience and saw Margaret's eyes clench whenever his name came up around others. Then she'd laugh. "Gave him up for climbing." Margaret let go of nonessentials, going through her climbing pack in the Purcell Range, tossing out a sweater, a fistful of rock gear, half her gorp. "Hasn't been used in the last three days. Gets dumped. Too burdensome." Yet on that trip Margaret pulled out dry mittens when Fay soaked hers.

Margaret, fitting her fingers into narrow cracks, slotting chocks as precisely as a surgeon, climbing the hard bits fast, placing her left foot, then the right, one time only. If Margaret could lead the pitch, Fay knew she could follow. They were the same size.

She hadn't called Joe after she found out. He wouldn't have asked her to come home, but just hearing his ordinary voice would have put an end to it.

Back in Talkeetna, when the notion not to go through with the climb struggled to surface, she had squashed it down. Stomped on it, as her kids would say. Because if she had paused to consider her options, like a rational human, she would have given the whole thing up. Now wasn't the time to come to grips with what had happened to Margaret. So all she had to do was keep on track, like a lioness out for a night's hunt, keeping to the scent, not letting in details that didn't pertain. She had never done anything like this. She wasn't a solo climber. But that was the thing: she didn't consider this a solo ascent.

▲ ▼ ▲

She crawled back from the crack and pushed up. Her knees had stiffened from kneeling too long. She stood in the alcove, took off her pack, and stowed her headlamp, which she had never turned on. "That was a damn fool thing, to climb without your light, Fay." Margaret's mother-hen tone. Fay saw Margaret's fingers rake off her hat and push through tangled black hair, through that central plume of snowy egret white.

Her right elbow ached and she pumped her arm once or twice, feeling the tendon resist. Below, a shadow welled, but far out on the Earth's rim heaved countless mountains, frosted peaks in pale pink rows.

She yawned in the cloudless dawn and shut her eyes, weary but strong after a night of climbing. She stretched, arms raised, standing at the mouth of the alcove. "I'm still good at this," she said aloud to Margaret.

After the avalanche they had backed off to the Wind Rivers, the Tetons, blaming their retreat on cranky knees, stiff wrists, reluctant elbows and shoulders. But this Alaskan mountain adhered to their minds like ice to rock.

She hunched on her pack and felt the crushing weight of the rope. Separately they had run their East and West Coast hills with packs of rocks, training for the fiftieth-birthday climb. Spent hours on the phone.

As she moved to the lip of the alcove she spotted the sling looped over a horn of rime-crusted rock. She knelt again and removed her pack. Bleached to dull rust, the sling was frayed and stiff and tore away lichen when she peeled it off. She held it in her gloved hands and time spun out again. Margaret was bending to sling the rock, rigging the rappel with her largest red sling, after the avalanche, when they were together again. Fay stuffed the sling in her pack. It smelled so cold here, like the inside of a meat locker. Her knees groaned when she pushed up with her palms.

Then she backed out of the alcove. Moved onto the snow slope, and adjusted her tools for climbing. She stood a moment on her front points, looking up, scanning the high slopes for safety, for a dark speck moving. The summer was dry, the snow well consolidated. The sun bounced off the snow's surface, blocking her vision. *Thunk, thunk.* Margaret was ahead, moving for the summit. And she was following.

▲ ▼ ▲

Margaret wasn't on the summit. She searched the sheltered side of the boulders. Margaret wasn't sprawled on the snow with the gorp bag open, hat askew, sweat beads like jewels on her upper lip, tan hand offering the canteen. "Drink, Fay, to another strong mountain!"

She let the wind push and tug and rattle her clothing. Her ungloved hand sprang out to ridges, vanishing into farther ridges, kaleidoscopic changes in the glittering light. She had never felt so alive.

Margaret must be behind, still on the route. In the darkness it was easy to pass her by. "That's logical, Fay." Margaret's soothing voice in the wind steadied her.

Her eyes smarted and she bit her knuckles. Her teeth chattered even though she was soaked in sunlight. That summer in the Cascades when every summit had been in clouds, Margaret had said, "What the hell, Fay, who said we climb just for the views?"

▲ ▼ ▲

They had planned to rappel and down-climb the route anyway. She couldn't possibly miss that snowy egret crest on the way down. She would have to guard against knocking off loose rocks, chunks of snow and ice, with Margaret below her now.

On the sixth rappel—she counted to keep her mind alert—the 'biner gate the rope passed through wavered. She watched it open and shut, open and shut, from the tension, like a wagging finger. She had forgotten to lock it. She hated rappelling.

She watched the rope slide around in the curve of the 'biner, gaining on the gate, backing off. She felt a white heat in her head that made the 'biner glisten a foot tall, remembering when Margaret fell down that snow slope in the Selkirks with nothing in. An easy slope. Fay had been taking in the view, paying out rope in a dreamy way. Then, out of the edge of her eye, she had caught Margaret shooting by, like a sack of laundry. She dug in her boots and braced herself, more as a way to pass the time than anything else. Her anchor wasn't up to this. Then her vision cleared and she could distinguish each snow crystal on her gloves as she let run a deliberate length of rope. Slowly, she clamped down the belay. "You hauled me out of the rinse/spin cycle," Margaret had hooted, safe, back in their tent, their thin voices shrill and high, six candles blazing.

▲  ▼  ▲

The high, bright light dimmed. The glacier was in shadow when her feet touched it, and there was a cold wind. The last light flicked over the summit. By now the wind up there had blown away her footprints.

She started walking toward the tent, feeling cold. Her jacket smelled of wet, metallic cold. She could see—yes!—a hand waving out of the tent door, jerking like red flagging in the bitter glacial wind.

Climbing! "As close as we'll come to flying," Margaret said after every climb. "Just like you New Englanders say every fall, 'I've never seen the foliage this beautiful!' "

"We mean it, always," Fay said.

"So do I," Margaret answered. They were in the tent on a mountain, drinking tea with sugar, cold fingers wrapped around warm cups and grinning like kids on Saturday.

A great darkness welled up, obscuring the glacier, ensnaring her feet. She was closer now, and saw steam from the cook pot wafting out the tent door.

*Professor Simon is in a coma,* the crushed-ice voice had said. Coma: a dark, hard land where move after move is at the limit of ability. Then an endless drop.

She was worn now. The ache in her knees made her stop in her tracks, and she pressed gloved hands to the sides of her face. She felt her eyes swell; then a stream was moving down her cheeks, over her chin, soaking her gloves. She was safe, but a panic rode in her throat. She began to run, smearing tears with her wet gloves, blinking back darkness, lurching toward the flapping tent.

# Interlude

# The First Ascent: A Story

by Guy Waterman

For the benefit of those readers who did not have time
to read Milton's *Paradise Lost* within the last year, some
background: the archangel Gabriel has been placed in
charge of the angels guarding Eden, where Adam and Eve
live in innocent bliss before their Fall. The fallen angel,
Satan, is known to have broken loose from Hell and to
intend evil toward the happy pair. Milton, like the Bible
before him, glosses over some of the details of the events
immediately preceding Satan's successful entry into Eden,
which are related somewhat more fully below. All quotations
in italics are verbatim from Book IV of *Paradise Lost.*

**Source:** The April 1980 issue of *Off Belay*.

▲ ▼ ▲

Gabriel sat betwixt the rocky pillars and watched two of the guards approaching along the base of the cliff. When the two young angels were within
about thirty feet of where Gabriel sat, they stopped and conversed in low
tones, examining the contours of the cliff, which rose sheer for two or three

hundred feet above them. Then one of the angels stepped up to the rock and stretched both arms forward, placing his hands carefully on a small crack that ran diagonally up to the left just over the level of his head. Gabriel could barely hear the low voice of the other angel, who was looking up at the rock just over the outstretched arms of his companion.

"You could go for the bucket up there on the left, but there's nothing for your feet at that point."

Gabriel got up and left his seat betwixt the pillars, walking slowly over to the two young angels. He looked up at the rock above them. The wall was very steep, even slightly overhung at the point where they stood, but the diagonal crack the first angel was gripping had sharp edges and led to a vertical crack that began about ten feet off the ground and ran up another six feet or so to where the angle of the cliff eased off a bit. A little way above that the crack ended in a narrow sloping ledge with a small cedar tree growing incongruously on it.

As Gabriel approached, the second angel quietly said, "Hi, chief," but the first one didn't notice his presence, so completely was he absorbed in the rock before him. Just as Gabriel reached the pair, the first angel stepped up onto small bumps just off the ground. In a couple of jerky motions, he moved his arms up and to the left, his hands grasping the sharp edges of the crack. He shifted his feet to the blank wall up and farther left. Then, pulling hard on the diagonal crack with his right hand, he reached tensely up high with his outstretched left, momentarily grabbed the base of the vertical crack, then slipped off and stumbled back against the second angel, who kept him from falling to the ground.

"That hold's not as good as it looks," said the first angel, not taking his eyes off the rock face that had just ejected him. "It's no bucket. Is that how Ithuriel did it?"

"I think so. I think maybe he got his left foot over on this sloping hold first."

Gabriel cleared his throat. "Say, are you fellows supposed to be on watch?"

"We just finished our shift, chief," said the second angel. "We were over on the northeast corner post. Everything seems to be quiet."

"What were you doing here?" said Gabriel, looking up at the rock.

The first angel rubbed his hands together and stepped back up to the diagonal crack. "We're trying to get up to that vertical line. This crack's got great holds to start, but there's not a thing for your feet . . . unless you could

get your left foot . . . " His voice trailed off as he studied minutely the rug-
osities of that sheer wall.

"It looks hard," commented Gabriel. "What do you do when you get to
the vertical crack? That gets awfully far off the ground. Has anybody got
that far?"

The first angel didn't answer, preoccupied, his hands gripping the diagonal crack, his right foot raised, trying different possible footholds just off the
ground.

"Ithuriel's got both hands on the vertical crack, but he was reluctant to
commit himself into the layback above," put in the second angel.

"That gets pretty high up, " said Gabriel. "Isn't there any way you could
protect it?"

"You could probably get stoppers in the vertical crack if you could let go
long enough to put anything in," replied the second angel, smiling.

Just then the first angel moved up on the diagonal crack again. He pro-
gressed a little more smoothly this time along the bottom moves. Then,
before trying to reach up with his left hand, he clung tight to the diagonal
crack and swung a left foot way, way out toward a vaguely sloping protru-
sion of smooth rock only a couple of inches square. His foot slipped off and
the angel dropped from his holds.

"Ithuriel's got to be kidding," he muttered.

Gabriel craned his neck to look farther up the craggy cliff that overhung
still as it rose beyond the ledge with the cedar tree at the top of the vertical
crack. "You know it's supposed to be impossible to climb anyway," he said
to the two angels. "I mean, that's why it's there, right? Wouldn't be much
security if just anyone could zip right up, would it?"

Neither of the angels said anything.

"Anyway, you've got better things to do than fool around and get yourself cracked up falling off rock. Why don't you join the others at some he-
roic games or something? I should get back to *my* post."

▲  ▼  ▲

Gabriel strode back to the alabaster pillars and sat down in the entrance
that wound up between them. The two angels stood a moment longer, studying the rock face before them, then walked slowly off, conversing in low
tones as before.

"Silly thing to be doing," thought Gabriel to himself. "Like to break their necks. Wonder who put them up to a thing like that?" He glanced back at the wall where the angel had been exerting himself a few moments before. As he looked, from this angle, he could see clearly the sharply edged diagonal crack slanting up to the base of the vertical crack, below which the wall seemed utterly blank and overhanging. "Crazy!" he muttered.

Then, as his eye zeroed in on the vertical crack, he noticed that only a few inches above where the diagonal crack joined it, there was a distinct widening of the vertical crack—a feature that was clearly visible from this angle but had not been perceptible from directly beneath.

"Hmmm . . . I wonder," thought the archangel reflectively. He started to get up to go back along the cliff, but then shook himself. "This is ridiculous," he snorted half aloud. "We're supposed to be guarding the place, not breaking in ourselves."

He sat down again and tried to keep his mind and his eyes off that section of the cliff. Another young angel passed by, carrying a harp limply in one hand, and nodded deferentially. The archangel acknowledged the greeting a bit more stiffly than usual.

After sitting rigidly, with eyes straight before him, for a good half hour, Gabriel stood up and stretched. He leaned against one of the alabaster pillars, looking the opposite direction from the diagonal crack, and tried to interest himself in some games in which half a dozen off-duty angels were exercising at a considerable distance away over a grassy field. He put out one hand to lean against the smooth pillar. As he did so, his hand happened to rest on a point where the otherwise unbroken surface of the pillar was varied by a kind of horizontal stratum about an inch wide, running along at shoulder height. As his hand felt this little obtrusion, the archangel looked around at it, then glanced higher to see if perhaps other imperfections might be observed higher up the pillar. Indeed, a kind of shallow groove presented itself, close to the right-hand edge of the pillar, and at the back of the groove the rock was jagged and bumpy. Gabriel's eyes surveyed this groove for some time, then dropped down and examined the lowest few feet of the pillar, where it ended in a succession of rounded stone extrusions.

With his left hand on the horizontal extrusion he had accidentally discovered, Gabriel stepped up on the lower stone extrusions, then reached up toward the groove with his right hand. He felt over several of the lumps and knobs at its back until he found one that seemed quite sharp, which he grabbed. Then, letting go of the horizontal hold with his left hand, he reached higher in the groove and found another hold. After he had worked himself up another couple of moves, he could get his left foot on the horizontal stratum that had been his original handhold. At that point he could find no further handholds above that suited him. He was stuck, his left foot placed awkwardly high on the horizontal hold, his right foot tenuously pushed against an indefinite bulge lower down, his right hand gripping tenaciously to a nubbin at the back of the groove, and his left hand feeling wildly above him. The groove seemed to flare outward more up there, and no hold could be found. He was breathing harder and grunting a bit, trying now to get a good lower hold with his left hand so he could try with his right, when a voice below him said, "Can you get your right knee up into the groove?"

Gabriel tumbled off the pillar and landed on the seat of his archangelic trousers on the ground at its base. Quickly springing to his feet, dusting off his hands, he looked around at a young stripling cherub who was grinning amiably at him from under a headful of curling blond locks that waved out from under a modest coronet.

▲ ▼ ▲

"You'd have had it if you could have got a knee up into the base of the groove," smiled the cherub, pointing with a silver wand that he bore in one hand.

"Knee?" snorted Gabriel contemptuously. Then, trying to regain some composure, he resumed his seat between the pillars and said with affected dignity, "And whose watch do you serve with, young man?"

The cherub grinned devilishly. "I'm a floater. Fill in whenever someone's absent." He leaned against the pillar, reached along the horizontal ledge Gabriel had used to start his moves, and looked sideways at the archangel.

"Well, I hope, when you have an opportunity to serve, that you take your watch seriously." Gabriel felt that he was sounding pompous, so he didn't go on, but sat trying to look preoccupied with important archangelic concerns.

The young cherub glided off down the cliff a bit and called back, "Have you tried this one here? It's quite interesting."

Gabriel looked around, annoyed. The cherub was standing at the sharp diagonal crack the two angels had been working on earlier that day. The archangel did not immediately answer, but, as he looked in that direction, his eye was attracted again to that spot where the vertical crack seemed to widen slightly.

The cherub called out cheerily, "I showed it to Ithuriel. He got quite well up into that vertical crack. I bet he'll get it after his watch today."

Gabriel tore his eyes off the cliff and glared at the young cherub. "I trust Ithuriel won't forget his first responsibilities." He stood up and stepped out from between the alabaster pillars.

"Do you think it would go?" asked the cherub sweetly.

Gabriel didn't answer, but his mind thought of that spot he had noticed from his seat between the pillars. He walked slowly over to the diagonal crack without looking at or saying a word to the young cherub. He reached out and ran his hands along the sharp edges of the diagonal crack. Great holds there, he thought. Then he gripped the two best spots he found, and stepped up onto the pathetically inadequate footholds below. He was surprised at how much the rock overhung, making the moves extremely strenuous despite the sharpness of the holds in the diagonal crack. Then he lunged quickly up with his left hand, aiming not for the base of the vertical crack, but for that hidden opening a little higher. His whole fist slotted into the fissure there, and he let out a satisfied grunt. With his left hand jammed hard into the vertical crack, he now moved first his left foot out onto the sloping hold the angels had pointed out before, then his right foot way up and out onto a part of the diagonal crack now behind and below him. Moving his right hand up high along the sharp left-hand edge of the vertical crack, he swung into a perfect layback, enabling him to release his weight from that left fist. Now he felt himself committed, but the vertical crack had really sharp edges on the left side, and there was just enough room for the feet out on the right to keep him moving up. Eventually he could sink his left toe into the opening that a moment before had given his left fist such a great jam hold. The angle of the crack eased off above that, and he was soon up on the ledge next to the cedar tree. There he sat down facing out, dangling his legs, swinging his tired arms, and puffing hard.

"Wow, that was terrific," called the youthful cherub below. "You looked very smooth."

Gabriel didn't answer. He looked around and noticed, for the first time, that it was possible to work his way along the ledge on which he was seated and gain the passage between the pillars, and thence return down the easy way. That made him recall that he had left the passage between the pillars unguarded during all this time, and he decided he'd better get back.

"That was really great," called the cherub from below. "What would you rate it?" Gabriel was weighing his answer when he heard a buzz of conversation and shuffling footsteps.

▲ ▼ ▲

A group of a dozen or so angels approached, bent in desultory conversation. This would be the next watch going to relieve their fellow angels, thought Gabriel. When they saw the cherub at the base of the cliff, they nodded in greeting. The young cherub smiled and pointed with his silver wand up at Gabriel seated on the ledge. The group of angels stopped and looked up, and immediately two of them stepped forward. Gabriel recognized them as the ones whom he had originally seen at this section of the cliff earlier in the day. The first of them said, "Hey, wonderful—did you get the move?"

The other joined in: "How hard was it?"

Gabriel felt good, but kept his voice low and relaxed: "Not too bad, really. There's a great jam for your left hand when you first go for the crack. You can slot your whole fist."

"Then what?" asked the first. "Go straight into a layback?"

Gabriel nodded.

"Ithuriel would flip his halo!" said the second angel.

The young cherub grinned fiendishly.

The first angel stepped up to the crack again and placed both hands on it, feeling for the best holds, his eyes intently studying the base of the vertical crack. "About six inches above the bottom?" he called up to Gabriel without taking his eyes off the crack.

Gabriel started to try to point it out to him from above, but then said he'd come down and show him.

The young cherub slid along the base of the cliff to the side of the first angel, where he stood at the diagonal crack. "Would you like to use some of this?" he asked in a low voice, holding out a blue cloth bag with the drawstrings pulled slightly open.

"What's that?" demanded the angel, momentarily distracted from his intense concentration on the rock before him. "Where'd you get that?"

"It makes your hands drier. You don't slip off the holds so much," replied the young cherub, smiling angelically.

"No, don't let Gabriel see you with that stuff," said the second angel. "It marks up the cliff something awful."

The cherub shrugged and moved off, saying something in an almost imperceptibly small voice about "it washes off after every rain."

The first angel, once more intent on the rock before him, carefully stepped up onto the bottom footholds, then moved swiftly and precisely up and left on the diagonal crack, then paused clutching there, readying himself for a lunge up at the vertical crack.

▲ ▼ ▲

"Wow, that's pretty good," said a third angel, stepping forward. "He's got those moves wired," said the second. "It's the next move that's tough. Ithuriel got it once this morning, but he couldn't get above that."

At that point the first angel stepped up as deliberately as he could manage and reached high with his left hand, aiming higher than he had that morning. He fumbled desperately at the base of the crack for about three seconds.

▲ ▼ ▲

Then his foot slipped from the wall and he crumbled down, muttering a mild angelic oath. "Almost had it . . . I got the hold . . . just wasn't high enough . . . " he mumbled.

The two other angels watched him, but the remainder of the group drifted off toward their watch assignments.

By this time Gabriel had joined them below. He was going to repeat the move for the benefit of the others, but when he saw the group of angels moving off, he hesitated. "You know, we really have to keep this watch going," he began. "I should be back at the pillars, and you men . . . "

The young cherub jumped up from where he had been sitting on the ground, his curly blond hair bobbing under his coronet. "I'll go watch the pillars, chief," he said sweetly. "You show Uzziel that move." Turning to the others, he went on, "You should have seen him do it. On sight too. Just went right up."

Gabriel still paused, but the young cherub had skipped off and was soon over between the pillars, where he looked back and smiled at them.

"What did you use for your left foot?" asked Uzziel.

"Uh . . . I'm not sure," said Gabriel absently looking from the cherub and the pillars back to the cliff face and the expectant looks of the three angels there. He stepped up and put his hands on the diagonal crack, feeling for the best holds. "I think I went up with the left hand before I moved my feet up."

He started up along the crack. He was conscious that he was not looking as smooth on the bottom moves as Uzziel had, having been over them only once before. They were harder than he recalled, the wall being so overhung at that point. Boldly he swung up for the vertical crack, aiming confidently for the fist jam. He got it, but not as securely as he had the first time. He was reluctant to move his feet up, not being quite so sure of his jam hold, so he hunched himself up a couple of times, trying to get his fist better lodged. Finally, he swung up on it, got his left foot neatly on the sloping hold below, and then reached way up with his right, going for the diagonal crack. The first time he didn't quite reach it and lurched awkwardly, almost coming off, and feeling tremendous strain on his left forearm and the fingers of his right hand. The second time he got his foot up. Then he got into the layback, but it took a terrible toll on his remaining arm strength before he finally worked high enough to sink his left foot into the jam hold at the base of the vertical crack and take some of the weight off his exhausted arms.

▲ ▼ ▲

Puffing hard, Gabriel stopped a moment there, shaking out first one hand and then the other. Aware that he had not looked very smooth at all, he tried to regain composure.

"That looks like some kind of a move," said Uzziel from below. One of the other angels let out a low whistle.

"It's not as bad as I made it look," said Gabriel, striving for a casual tone but still breathing hard. Leaning back on the sharp holds of the vertical crack, he looked up, studying the bulge above the ledge. "You know," he said, "that part up there just might go." The others stepped out from the base and craned to look above him. Again one of them whistled.

"Does it look like you could get any protection in?" asked one of the other angels, not Uzziel.

"That might be the problem . . . unless . . . there's a kind of a crack . . . " Gabriel's voice trailed off as he peered intently at the cliff above him.

From off to his right, and a little above him, came a voice: "Maybe you could put in a bolt." Gabriel looked around sharply. From over where the ledge met the pillars—where Gabriel had descended after his first climb up—the face of the youthful cherub was peering around at him, smiling wickedly.

"Are you watching that entrance?" said Gabriel, a trifle irritably.

"Don't worry, I'll watch it. Nothing'll get in here," called the cherub and withdrew back behind the nearer pillar.

Gabriel finished the last moves up the crack and turned to go back along the ledge toward the pillars.

"How does it look from there? Could you put anything in?" Uzziel was calling from below.

Gabriel carefully turned around on the ledge. He studied the rock above him for a full two minutes, leaning up and out as much as he dared. When he finally stepped back, he called to the others below, "Listen, I really think that would go. Maybe tomorrow I might give it a try."

"Who's going to follow you, though?" chuckled Uzziel. "You'd have to haul me over the first move, and then I sure would be too shot for the bulge."

As Gabriel worked himself across the ledge to the descent between the pillars, his mind was preoccupied with the intricacies of what he had seen above the cedar tree on the ledge. As he came down the easy access between the pillars, the young cherub smiled sweetly at him from his seat on a rock. Gabriel nodded back, not smiling. Something about this cherub made him uneasy.

As he got to the bottom again and turned to rejoin the angels, he saw that Ithuriel and another angel had joined the other three, apparently on their return from being relieved of the watch. As Gabriel walked back toward them along the cliff, he watched with some satisfaction, as Uzziel was talking quickly and gesturing up at the vertical crack while Ithuriel and the other angel listened closely and gazed at the rock above them.

When they noticed Gabriel approach, Ithuriel turned and burst into a big grin: "That's great, chief. That's some move. I got as far as that vertical crack this morning, but it looked like it didn't let up above that."

"It's not really so bad," said Gabriel, smiling faintly. "Hello, Xephon."

Ithuriel's companion nodded, also smiling. "Hi. Quite a move, chief. Do you think one of us can get it?"

"Oh, sure you can," said Gabriel quickly. "You both can."

Ithuriel put down a spear and turned toward the rock. He moved elegantly up the first moves, then without hesitation swung his left foot out onto the high sloping hold before reaching up from the diagonal crack. From that awkward stance, he went up with his left hand and seized the lower end of the crack—not Gabriel's jam hold—and then moved his right foot up to a small nubbin just below the diagonal crack. It seemed to Gabriel incredible that Ithuriel could stay on such small holds without benefit of that big jam hold.

"If you can get just a little higher," he couldn't help saying amid the silence of the other angels. "Your left hand just a little higher. It's a real bucket."

But Ithuriel wasn't hearing him. His left arm was obviously straining hard to hold him on, as he let go with the right and went desperately for a higher hold. A few moments of precarious struggling and he was up to where he could get his weight off his arms.

"Terrific!" breathed Xephon from below.

Ithuriel let out a whoop. "Wow, some move. I thought sure I was coming off, I'm telling you."

"So did we," said Xephon.

"Real good, Ithuriel," said Gabriel quietly. "I don't see how you could get it without using that fist jam."

Ithuriel let out another whoop. From his resting position, he threw back his head and looked up at the bulge that arched over the cedar tree on the ledge. "Hey, chief, do you really think that bulge would go? It looks very interesting."

"If you're game, I'd have a go at it tomorrow," said Gabriel, also studying the cliff above. "It would be quite a route. All depends on whether we could get protection in."

"We?" chortled Ithuriel. "I'm not leading that thing! I'd sure second you, though, if you want to go fall off it."

Uzziel spoke quietly, standing beside Gabriel: "Would you like to borrow my rack? I could run back up and get it after watch tonight."

Gabriel considered a moment. "Maybe that would be good, if you didn't mind. But, say . . . you know . . . don't say anything about this to Michael, OK?"

"Sure," replied Uzziel. Gabriel glanced at him and saw that he was smiling. Half smiling back, and looking back at the cliff he went on, "I just mean . . . you know . . . he'd be just likely to come busting down here at dawn and try to go at it. He's so awfully competitive, that Michael."

Uzziel snickered. "I know what you mean. Sure, chief, I won't say a word to a soul."

Gabriel felt a little embarrassed and looked hard at the rock. Ithuriel was finishing the easy moves to the ledge.

▲  ▼  ▲

Looking up, Gabriel had not been aware of the approach of another figure till just then. When he looked around, he felt simultaneous surprise, embarrassment, and a bit of mild annoyance at the unexpected arrival of fellow archangel Uriel. While the lesser angels at the base of the cliff fell silent and stepped back a pace, the two archangels exchanged a fairly formal greeting. While Uriel did not directly ask what all this activity was about, Gabriel felt distinctly on the defensive and asked rather stiffly what brought the regent of the sun to this earthly quarter.

Uriel said:

*"Gabriel, to thee thy course by lot hath given. Charge and strict watch that to this happy place No evil thing approach or enter in."*

"Of course. This is the off-duty watch, you understand," said Gabriel, aware that at least a couple of the angels present were really of the watch then supposed to be on duty. "Everything's well watched." He thought uncomfortably of that young cherub that had agreed to hold his spot between the pillars and wished he could see him now from where he and Uriel were standing.

Uriel nodded soberly and went on in that curiously stilted way of talking that he had:

*"This day at highth of noon came to my sphere A spirit, zealous, as he seemed, to know More of the Almighty's works, and chiefly man God's latest image: I described his way. Bent on all speed, and marked his airy gait."*

Gabriel listened uneasily. "Anything unusual about him?"

Uriel continued:

*"But in the mount that lies from Eden north, where he first lighted, soon discerned his looks Alien from heaven, with passions foul obscured: Mine eye pursued him still, but under shade Lost sight of him . . . "*

Gabriel frowned. "Just north of here? Wish you had let us know earlier. Have any ideas as to who it might be?"

Uriel pressed both hands together, looked at the ground a moment, then back to his fellow archangel, his eyebrows raised.

*"One of the banished crew, I fear, hath ventured from the deep, to raise New troubles; him thy care must be to find."*

Gabriel was distinctly uncomfortable now. "What did you say this fellow looked like?" he asked rather sharply.

Uriel thought a moment, then responded:

*"A stripling cherub he appears, not of the prime, yet such as in his face Youth smiled celestial, and to every limb suitable grace diffused, so well he feigned; Under a coronet his flowing hair in curls on either cheek played; wings he wore of many a colored plume sprinkled with gold, His habit fit for speed succinct, and held Before his decent steps a silver wand."*

Gabriel glanced impulsively at the pillars and his first tendency was to run back there to find that cherub. Coronet . . . curls . . . silver wand . . . he thought to himself, a terrible foreboding coming over him. Still, he didn't want to go to the trouble of explaining to Uriel all the background of what had been happening and how he came to let the young cherub occupy his place between the pillars. It would sound bad at first. Anyway, he thought, chances are that that cherub is sitting right there where he was a minute ago. As soon as Uriel goes, I'll get over there and have a talk with him.

Uriel saw Gabriel's preoccupation and tactfully took his leave, wished him well, and the next moment was gone. Trying not to look hurried, and ignoring a question from Xephon, who was standing at the diagonal crack, Gabriel strode back toward the pillars. As he came round into the entrance, Ithuriel was coming down the easy rock, having traversed across the ledge from the cedar tree. No other being was visible.

"Where's that cherub?" demanded Gabriel, looking past Ithuriel.

"What cherub, chief? Who?" asked Ithuriel.

Gabriel's heart sank. "Oh boy," he muttered. He stood a moment, staring up between the pillars, as the full import of the situation sank in. Almost simultaneously with that realization, he began to think quickly what needed doing now. Rushing in on his consciousness was the thought that he had little daylight left. Already the shadows crept halfway up the cliff face. They would likely be doing most of their search in the dark, thought Gabriel, unless we act real fast and are lucky, luckier than I deserve—but that last sentiment scarcely lingered a second. His mind now focused on the needed action.

"What is it, chief?" asked Ithuriel, concern showing clearly in his open face.

Gabriel wheeled about and called to the others. He instructed one of the angels to round up the off-duty angels on the double and get them all back here to the pillars fast. He ordered Uzziel to wait till all those angels were assembled and armed, and gave him rapid instructions where to meet him. Then he barked to Ithuriel and Xephon to follow him and started quickly up between the pillars. Xephon grabbed Ithuriel's spear and tossed it to him, and both angels followed their leader's course.

It was a bad night. Gabriel's worst fears proved true. After searching virtually all night, they discovered the intruder. Ithuriel and Xephon found him in the garden itself—but not in the form of the youthful cherub who had passed the afternoon with them. Angry words were exchanged. Blows might have followed, but the enemy suddenly fled murmuring. And with him fled the shades of night.

It was dawning gray and bleak as Gabriel and his band returned dispiritedly down toward the pillars where they had only the afternoon before enjoyed such pleasant hours. As they came wearily out at the base of the pillars, Gabriel remembered the rock face and his mind grabbed eagerly on a subject that took him away from feelings of guilt and dread of what would be said of him after his allowing the intruder to get by his defenses. He found it easy to let his mind run over the satisfaction of having mastered that first twenty feet or so—and the prospects of leading that hard bulge ahead. Not today, of course, after having been up all night. Not till this nasty business was all settled and things had quieted down somewhat. On the other hand, he sure wouldn't want Michael coming down and beating him to it. Michael was so competitive, it would be like him to . . .

Ithuriel's voice next to him broke in on his reveries: "Still want to take a crack at that climb, chief? Remember, I'll be glad to second you."

Gabriel smiled, feeling warmly toward this good friend, who would work so hard with him all night, then come to the same thoughts as soon as their serious business was over. "Let's have a look," he said, and the two began to wander slowly toward the diagonal crack.

As they did so, they heard a noise from up on the cliff, and a moment later a voice calling, "Fifteen feet." A couple of seconds later, from much farther up in the air, another voice answered, "Almost up."

Gabriel and Ithuriel looked at each other and walked faster till they got out from the cliff a ways. Up on the face about halfway, a slender figure stood perched on a small ledge underneath a bulge of dark rock. From him a thin strand of rope could be traced all the way to where it disappeared over the very top of the cliff. Just as they looked, a head and pair of shoulders appeared looking down the rope.

"Who is it, can you tell?" said Ithuriel tensely beside him.

"I think . . . oh no, it's Him," murmured Gabriel.

As he spoke, the voice from the cliff called, "Off belay, Son."

The slender figure on the ledge called back up the cliff, "Belay off, Father."

# THE REVELA-TION AND THE RE-MAINING UNRE-VEALED

# The Meaning and the Enduring Mystery of Climbing to Diverse and Diverging Climbers

Why climbers climb is a question on which more fatuous nonsense has been wasted than perhaps any question since one of Socrates' puzzlers. For many a supple acrobat threading a delicate web of tenuous holds high on an airy precipice, and for many a high-altitude mountaineer ducking an ice-encrusted parka hood before screaming winds, the only explanation necessary is the sheer ecstasy of being where most people will never be. If that ecstasy appears incomprehensible, nonsensical to us, that makes not a particle of difference to them. Theirs is still the joy. No explanation owed.

Maybe the reason is the same reason why the businessman strives to corner a market, why the tenor goes for those seven high C's, why the politician runs for another election, why the social worker goes to work in a dangerous part of town, why the dairy farmer girds for another year of diminishing sales and rising costs. The challenge demands response. Yes, because it's there. This can be as mundane as the handyman (or handywoman) undertaking to refinish an old desk, or as grippingly serious as Ahab going after the White Whale, or Satan setting out from Hell to subvert mankind, or Antigone hell-bent to bury her brother. Maybe, with so much at stake on the mountain, climbers feel a closer kinship to Ahab and Antigone than to the handyman with the sander in his hand. For some climbers the explanation may seem even more trivial. It's just fun to move up ten feet on tiny holds. Or the sunset at fourteen thousand feet takes your breath away. Or the quiet hills bring respite after five days of rush-hour traffic and a hectic office.

For a few the stakes seem higher: the mountains (and maybe also the polar regions, and maybe also the wide expanses of the largest open seas) stand as this abused planet's last refuge of wildness. The Thoreauvian cliché about wildness preserving the world is subject to anyone's interpretation, but there are plenty of people who feel that the more relentlessly we bring our order and culture to the natural world, the more we risk the final loss of that priceless one-to-one experience with the wild.

In the stories that follow, you'll join Charles Fay and Bob Collin and the Lorax as they strive to preserve their particular vision of something like wildness. You may prefer to see people simply responding reflexively to challenge on a greater or smaller scale. Or maybe, like the kids badgering Michelle to come climbing with them, you may not know exactly what it is. But you know it's important.

# THE DEATH OF PASSA-CONAWAY

**R**esearch for our historical mountain writings introduced us to the charming figure of Charles Ernest Fay—and to the challenging question he posed and mulled over a century ago and more. Professor Fay identified a quandary, set forth both in what he wrote and even more vividly in what he did in 1891. When we published our own musings on the same issues 102 years later, we chose Fay's quandary as the starting point. The excerpt that follows served as the first chapter and keynote for our book *Wilderness Ethics*.

**Source:** *Wilderness Ethics*.

▲ ▼ ▲

**More than a century ago, on October 7, 1891, Professor Charles Ernest Fay of Tufts** University read a paper before a gathering of Boston's then fifteen-years-old Appalachian Mountain Club. In that faded document of a bygone era lies a text suitable for thinking about today.

Professor Fay was a small but spry climber who loved the wild side of the mountains. As a young man he went overseas for the usual summer climbing seasons in the Alps, obligatory for aspiring alpinists of his day. But when he got back home, he would head for the White Mountains of New Hampshire. He seemed to find more genuine mountain wildness in the little-known corners of these forested hills. During the 1870s and 1880s, before there were a lot of hiking trails in the White Mountains, Professor Fay delved into many a hidden ravine and thrashed through thickets to many a summit where few had been before. Where difficulties lay, there he was happiest.

When trails were built in those hills, he turned to the Canadian Rockies for adventure. In that wilderness of unclimbed peaks, beginning when he was nearly the age of fifty, he made explorations and first ascents of such notable summits as Victoria, Lefroy, and Dawson. Highly respected by his contemporaries, he served several terms (which was unusual) as president of both the Appalachian Mountain Club and the American Alpine Club, the dominant mountain societies of that generation. Canada named a good-size mountain after him.

The bespectacled and bewhiskered face that peers out at us from faded old mountaineering journal photos conveys a spirit of humor as well as adventure. Most nineteenth-century visages look grim today. Who would want to go hiking with Ulysses Grant or Johannes Brahms? But Professor Fay is someone you'd want to have known, to have strolled a leaf-strewn trail with, to have joined as he was sitting on the barren scree slopes of Mount Lefroy sipping a cup of tea before making the first ascent.

Just before he went west, Professor Fay stood face to face with a quandary. We are fortunate that he aired his feelings in that paper read to the AMC gathering in Boston more than a hundred years ago.

▲ ▼ ▲

Fay's quandary was met on Mount Passaconaway, a graceful 4,060-foot wooded summit, the highest point in the Sandwich Range, that southern-most tier of the White Mountains. Fay first knew Passaconaway as a trail-less mystery, "gloomy and ponderous." "In my youth it seemed to me of massive iron," he recalled, and was suffused with "the interest which attaches to the unknown." Until the summer of 1891 "it may be doubted whether a score of persons had ever found their way to its summit."

A few weeks after his second climb of this peak, a tumultuous wind broke over the region, concentrating its fury on the upper slopes of Passaconaway. The open woods that Fay had enjoyed became a "wreck-age" of downed timber. The difficulty of reaching the top following that windstorm, combined with a local campaign to build more hiking trails, persuaded Professor Fay to cut a trail to the top of Mount Passaconaway.

After fruitless reconnaissances of other possibilities, Fay's party elected to start the trail at the end of an abandoned wood road to a deserted saw-mill, "Dicy's" (today rendered "Dicey's Mill"). Not only did they cut a trail, with considerable difficulty in scouting the route through the upper-elevation blowdown, but they also erected a simple log shelter, nine feet by four-teen feet, seven feet high in front, sloping to three feet in back, and heaped inside with fragrant hemlock boughs. (Today you don't see hemlock anywhere near that high on the peak; perhaps the boughs were balsam fir? Professor Fay's professional field was Romance languages, not botany.)

At the end of several days' hard work, Professor Fay stood back to ad-mire the handiwork of their "Passaconaway Lodge" and to contemplate the new-cut trail, which now made the once "gloomy and ponderous" peak into "a comfortable one day's trip for such as had no more time to devote to it." He recalled, "The sun was flooding all this with evening glory as we finished our work."

Surely this scene was cause for deep satisfaction, a rich sense of accom-plishment, of opening up that lovely mountainside to be shared by such as had never been there before.

And yet . . . at this point Professor Fay began to reflect. What had they done?

> Was it justifiable to love the mountain not less, but climbers
> more? As one of the limited number to whom its secrets
> had been revealed, was it or not a breach of confidence to
> plan for the wholesale invasion of its privacy, and to aid in
> making it a readily accessible peak?

▲  ▼  ▲

He thought of the wood road to the site of Dicy's mill, which local folks had promised to upgrade to provide easier access to the base of the new trail. "Another season will no doubt see a carriage-road as far as 'Dicy's,' " he mused mournfully. "May no season ever see it carried farther; for whoever would not prefer to go from there to the summit by his own effort is not worthy to set foot on Passaconaway."

He thought of the viewpoints that had been cleared on the wooded sum-mit—one on the east side, cut by another early bushwhacker, Frank Bolles, "whose love of wild nature had now and then led him to this secluded spot," and one on the northwest, cut by his own party. On the true summit, others had thought to clear a southward view by "much labor and ruthless destruction of fine trees," but Fay had prevailed on them to desist, and instead to select "a tall spruce with branches conveniently set for climbing," which they furnished with "an improvised ladder." If anyone needed a view from the very top, let them exert the added effort and ingenuity of climbing another fifteen feet for it. Leave the trees alone. They were there first. They live there, people just visit. Professor Fay, though he seemed not to know the difference between hemlock and balsam fir, believed that trees had rights too.

By the light, first, of a dwindling campfire and, later, of a harvest moon, Professor Fay sat up all night at Camp Passaconaway. "It was too glorious a night to sleep," he reported. Perhaps he was seeking, in the novelist Ellen Glasgow's words, "to preserve, within a wild sanctuary, an inaccessible valley of reveries."

In the morning they broke camp, the party fully expecting to descend with pride their new-cut trail. Instead Professor Fay announced they would bushwhack down over the Wonalancet Ridge. Back into the jumble of blowdown, over the uneven mossy terrain of rocks and downed logs, and on down the steep slope, the puzzled party followed the intrepid Charles Ernest Fay.

Why the bushwhack down? Wrote Fay in his paper before the AMC, "To prolong the luxury of the forest to the last possible moment."

That is a fine sensibility that finds "luxury" in the untamed forest, not the cleared path; in the difficult way, not the easy; the road less traveled by, which makes all the difference. Would that we could have tripped behind Professor Fay as he thrashed through the thickets and down the Wonalancet Ridge, disdaining the new-cut trail that he himself had conceived and directed a hundred years ago.

What was Fay doing? Can we learn from him?

On one level, the answer is that Professor Fay was savoring the yet-untamed wildness of the mountain. In spite of the new trail and the sheltering roof, the mountain's wildness remained yet untamed, providing only that those who valued that wildness would seek it out. That was his message to his puzzled companions in the 1890s, and it is equally Professor Fay's message to us in the twenty-first century. Our mountains have many more trails and many more sheltering roofs than Professor Fay's did, but we can yet preserve that spirit of wildness, provided that we value the wildness, savor it, and do what we must to preserve it for this century and centuries to come as well.

But, as Professor Fay recognized in warning against extending the carriage road beyond Dicy's and in ruling against cutting summit trees, that wildness is fragile. We can lose it, we can be agents of its destruction, if we are not wise and caring stewards. The key is to decide where our values lie. It is fun to enjoy the easy trail and the sheltering roof. But if we indulge ourselves too much in bringing civilized comforts, do we not destroy qualities that originally brought us to the mountain? Is it not better to savor the wildness, to throw ourselves into the very uncomfortableness of the untamed thickets, to "prolong the luxury of the forest"?

Professor Fay wanted to share the mountain experience: that's why he built the trail and shelter on Passaconaway, and that's why he helped form and lead the Appalachian Mountain Club. But he also recognized that the essence of the mountain experience is challenge, difficulty, reaching the inaccessible, rising to heights you haven't achieved before. When he mused over the results of his work on Passaconaway, he was contemplating an important question: Just what is it we're trying to share? The experience of being on top of the mountain? Or the experience of climbing to get there and *then* being there, in an altogether richer spirit? Do we really do anyone favors by smoothing the way? Or, in our patronizing, self-aggrandizing role as trail builder and shelter provider, do we impoverish the mountain experience for those we set out to help?

What values matter most to us? In an increasingly urbanized society, surrounded by technological marvels in our everyday lives, why do we value the mountains? Are they a sanctuary where we preserve a special kind of experience to savor? Or are they merely a recreational gymnasium for our off-hours? Aren't they something more?

Half a century later, and a hundred miles to the west, another who loved to share the mountains, Russell M. L. Carson of the Adirondacks, expressed his concern:

> In all our thinking about recreational development, we
> ought constantly to remember that wilderness and natural

beauty are the real charm of the Adirondacks, and that preservation is as much our objective as helping more people to share our joy in them.

▲  ▼  ▲

Professor Fay sought to preserve, to savor, and he set an example to his companions and to us. As trail builder and hiker, he sought the right balance between sharing and preserving. He built the trail, but he urged no carriage road. He cut an outlook, but he required his summit visitor to climb a bit more (on that spruce with "conveniently set" branches) to see the view. He took satisfaction in the trail and shelter he'd built, but when he had thought about it, he elected to descend by a pathless way "to prolong the luxury of the forest to the last possible moment."

What Professor Fay wrestled with on Mount Passaconaway in 1891, we all confront today. What are we building? What are we trying to preserve? What is happening to the backcountry?

The underlying question more than a hundred years later, not only in the Sandwich Range or the White Mountains, and not just through all the mountain ranges of the world, but in varied forms throughout the surface of this crowded globe, is whether the spirit of wildness is facing its "last possible moment." The question is whether, and specifically how, we may prolong the "luxury" of having the quality of mountain experience that Professor Fay knew and loved so well.

Fay's quandary is ours.

# REACH-ING FOR THE F***ING STARS

## A STORY

by Laura Waterman

**W**hen we were researching *Yankee Rock & Ice* during the mid-1980s, Shawangunk climbers told us that one group we really had to talk to were a bunch of kids who were climbing harder than anyone ever had in the Northeast, but using radically new methods, some of which their elders thoroughly disapproved. As elders ourselves, we fully expected to find these kids hard to take: brash, self-promoting, heedless of old values, and most likely hostile to questions from middle-aged has-beens writing a book, probably a dull one. We could not have been more off the mark. For three hours the "kids" eagerly plied us with their views on modern climbing; their enthusiasm, verve and goodwill; their delight that someone from the older generation would listen to (and take notes on!) their accomplishments as well as their vision of where the future of climbing lay. They played the role of goodwill ambassadors from a strange new world.

Much later (mid-1990s), Laura set out to capture in fiction the exuberance, the excitement, and the infectious crudity of this generation, inarticulate as to what climbing meant to them, but convinced that it was the cornerstone of their lives. In everyday talk, our own language is squeaky-clean. So Guy was astonished to learn some new four-letter words from Laura's prose. He had only just expanded his horizon from "darn" and "heck" to "damn" and "hell," and here she was presenting some further four-letter innovations. We hope readers will agree that these characters just talk like this, and any dialogue that cleaned up the language would be hopelessly unrealistic.

**Source:** Spring 1997 issue of *U.S. 1 Worksheets.*

▲ ▼ ▲

**"Jesus, Michelle, you'll feel like air up there, like a goddamn piece of air," Tony says as** I plunk down three beers at The Kids' table. That's what I call them in my head, since most of the time they act like my eight-year-old brother.

"We keep telling you, Michelle, you got a rock climber's build," Astroman says, then turns to the others, "Look at her hand size, will ya?" He holds up his own mitt, which resembles a meat cleaver. "If I had her fingers I'd work that narrow crack on *Boomerang,* no prob." He grins up at me, waggling fingers as thick as cucumbers. They're taped to protect them from rock bites, but his knuckles are scraped and he's torn the scabs off the back of his hands. All their hands look like they're in the last stages of leprosy.

The one they call Beanbag is resting his elbows on the table, twitching his forearm muscles like a boa constrictor digesting a rodent. I can make my forearms do that too, from hefting endless trays of burgers, fries, brews.

"Hey, Bean, how about those reachy moves on *Staircase to Starland* yesterday?" Tony cackles. "Betcha Michelle could cruise them." He turns to Astro, "Old Bean got off route onto loose rock and lichen trying to dodge that spot."

"Fucking rush, man." Bean is bulging out his eyes.

All the climbers who wind up at the Off Belay Café talk like that. "Maaaan," I hear as I approach a table, "when I came around the corner and saw that overhang I almost pissed. It was two body-lengths long, I'm telling you." Or, "Peeled thirty feet on a shitty number-one Stopper." It took a while, but I've caught on to their lingo now. Or, "I was pumped. Then my protection popped, but, Holy Christ, I was committed." The guy who says that hee-haws insanely. If you saw a person coming at you on the sidewalk laughing like that, you'd cross the street. It's crossed my mind many times as I bring them burgers and beers: am I looking at the rest of my life?

▲ ▼ ▲

I wipe off The Kids' table, dole out hamburgers and fries. Tony and Astro start jabbering at me, jumping around in their seats. They're imitating climbing moves, but to me they look like gorillas on the high bars.

"How'ja like to look down on the treetops, Michelle?"

"Tiny tufts of green shag," Astro says. "You wouldn't believe what it's like."

"You and *space*," Tony chants.

"Climbing higher." Astro flicks Tony's arm,

"Power surge—the top, aaaaaaah." Tony's got one foot on top of the table, throws up his arms, head tossed back, grinning at the ceiling. Then folds back into his seat. "Hmmmmm, rock. Feels good on a sunny day."

"Good, uuummmfff, for you, too," Bean mumbles, wolfing down his burger.

"How about it, Michelle?" Tony grabs my arm. "Look, guys, great strength-to-weight ratio, huh? I bet we couldn't pump trays like she does for eight hours. Wadda workout!" He lifts my arm for them to gawk at. "Real potential. Can'tja see her swarm that thin section on *Head Trip?* Hey, Michelle," he's grinning in my face. "You'd crank those long reaches like a spider."

"Let go, Tony. I'm working, in case you didn't notice." I'm wrestling Tony for my arm, but his fingers are wrapped around it like kudzu vine. The other two are laughing, cradling their beers. "I'm my baby's sole means of support, so forget it." That's not strictly true. I live with my mother. She's baby-sitting right now since I'm at work. She lets me know once a day I haven't finished high school and I've already ruined my life. She tells me climbers are juvenile, but I don't tell her I agree.

"Whoa, Spiderwoman," Tony screeches, waving my arm. "Wait till we get you on the rock."

I ball my fist and ram it toward his nose. He swerves, but still I score, plowing into his cheekbone.

He drops my arm. "Cut it out, Michelle. That hurt!"

"Then leave me alone." My knuckles sting, but I keep myself from rubbing. That would only encourage them.

"Ooooooh, Tony got smacked," Astro giggles.

Beanbag gets caught midswallow. He gasps, inhales, coughs, and a spew of beer spurts out his mouth, splatting their body-builder shirts, soaking Tony's hamburger.

"Gross, Bean." Tony's voice gets tough-loud, a face-saving tactic.

I fling my cloth down on the table—they can clean this mess up—and move on to more climbers wanting beer and burgers.

I would never tell them that the other reason I wouldn't try climbing is I can still remember kids yelling, "Aiiiiii, here comes Spiderwoman," then running like hell from the tallest skinniest person in the class, by far. I'd slink off to find a tree to hide behind. Never have found a good place for these long arms and legs.

▲ ▼ ▲

"We'd have you climbing 5.9 the first day, Michelle." Tony's like my mother; he can't lay off.

"Make ya feel . . . ooooooooooh," Astroman raises his arms skyward as I set down more beers.

"Like you could touch the fucking *stars*," Bean says. He breathes in and expands his chest, which seems to fill the room.

"Wow! That's poetic, man. Old Bean's a poet." Tony flings back his head and cackles. Then his face goes serious and he leans toward the others, shutting me out, though I keep standing there, listening. "Goddamn, Bean's right." Tony's voice is breathy, as though he's just figured something out. "I never would have gone to college if I'd never gone climbing."

Astro nods, his eyes locked into Tony's. "Me, too," he says. "I'd still be setting up pins at the bowling alley. Weird, huh?"

"Naaaa," Bean says.

Tony and Astro gaze at Bean, who's leaning back in his seat, his muscled arms folded across his chest. Arms it takes years on rock to make.

All three start nodding, heads close together, as though they're exchanging some born-again secret password.

I've got tables waiting, but I break in, "Huh! Pretty soon you'll tell me

Bean's going to med school." But they don't hear a word.

"Remember Conrad when he first came to the cliffs?" Tony says.

"Yeah, that geeky kid looked sideways at his shoes if you said, 'How's it going, Conrad, man,'" Astro's voice is hushed the way you talk in church.

"Then we heard old Conrad's on-sighting 5.12," Tony says.

"Right. And it's, like, now he can look you in the eye forever," Astro says.

"Working out hard moves a hundred feet off the deck can freshen up your life totally," Tony says.

"Hey, they don't have to be that hard. Just being on rock does it," Bean says. "But *you'll* never know, Michelle." He's looking up at me.

"Know what?"

"What we're talking about."

"Cut the gab, Michelle." I flinch. My boss's voice can break into my brain at the precise wrong moment, like my mother's.

"Until you try," Tony says.

"Climbing? You think *I've* got a screw loose?"

"Michelle!" OK, boss. I make my feet move away from them, telling myself how foul-mouthed climbers are, caroming around in oversize egos like nine-year-olds driving Jaguars.

▲ ▼ ▲

"So, where do ya live, Michelle? We'll pick you up tomorrow morning," Tony says as I bring them the check. "Your day off, right?" He's staring at the check, like he's double-checking the addition, but I know he's playing it casual, hoping this time to mouse-trap me.

"My mother's working tomorrow. I have to stay home with the baby."

"Fuck the baby," Astro says.

"Bring the baby," Bean says.

We all stare at Bean, who grins and flings his arms open. I see more muscle, but they're nowhere near as long as mine.

"Yeah! Bean loves babies." Tony's pounding the table, making the glasses dance.

I hear my mother's voice: "You did *what?*"

I reach the full length of the table for the money Tony's holding. "Bet you could tie your shoes without bending over, Michelle." But he's careful to keep his eyes off my arm.

"Flora Park," I say. Which makes the other two look like they've just cruised that overhang two body-lengths long and landed in med school. "You know where that is?"

"Sure," Tony says, examining the check, which is lying on the table. "Be at the mailboxes at eight."

I pick up the check, curling it and the bills into my palm, tightening my fingers. As I walk over to the cash register, I squeeze my fist in and out, in and out, sending a power surge up my forearm.

# CAN WOMEN LEAD ON ICE?

## LEARNING BY THE PROCESS OF DEFAULT

**B**ack around a generation ago, when I (Laura) started climbing, no women were leading hard climbs; none that I heard about, anyway. For sure no women back then were leading at the top of the day's standard; certainly not at the Gunks, where I learned to climb. In the 1940s and 1950s, Bonnie Prudden had helped set standards at the Shawangunks, sharing leads on first ascents with Fritz Wiessner and Hans Kraus. Maria Millar and Krist Raubenheimer also led on rock, putting in the occasional new route. But by the time I came along in the late 1960s, they were just names in the guidebook, and the day of Barbara Devine, Rosie Andrews, and Lynn Hill was far in the future.

As for ice, I had never heard of a woman in the Northeast leading ice at all. Very, very few even followed it. On the many occasions when Guy and I went up to Chapel Pond or Huntington Ravine, I can scarcely ever recall another woman going to the top of the Big Slab or staying at the Harvard Cabin. Lonely times.

I just tell you these bare facts to set the scene for what

follows. The phrase "role model" was not in our vocabulary then. I would have given a lot for some strong ice woman to look up to. Such a one would have had a big influence on me and shortcut my stumbling path in quest of leading on ice myself. But, then, if such a creature had existed, the tale I'm about to tell would not have happened in quite the same way.

**Source:** Adapted from *Yankee Rock & Ice.*

▲ ▼ ▲

**I started climbing ice in 1970, just missing the torturous step-cutting age and** just in time to grasp Chouinard's revolutionary first-generation drooped picks.

Every weekend, leaving Friday after work, Guy (who wasn't yet my husband) and I drove four wintry hours up to the Adirondacks. We routinely set up our tent on Chapel Pond, securing it with deadly old Marwa ice screws. (They were nicknamed "coat hangers" because they were as effective as coat hangers at catching falls, as was proved by Dan Doody and Craig Merrihue on a sad day in Pinnacle Gully. That's why we used these screws for attaching our tent to the ice on Chapel Pond, *not* for climbing.) We would pound them in with our new Chouinard alpine hammers and be comfortably settled in our sleeping bags before midnight.

The next day's early light might reveal four or five other tents on the pond's solid surface. We were all ice climbers from the New York area who during the warm months climbed rock together at the Gunks. All of us had speeded through Friday night to be in the right position to use well those bounteous floes around Chapel Pond.

I didn't pay much attention to the fact that I was about the only woman interested in climbing ice—regularly, that is. Some of the women I knew from the Gunks might come for a weekend or two, but they didn't stay. It was nothing new for me. In those days there were always more men than women at climbing areas. Anyway, as a kid I had grown up playing with the boys.

I climbed with Guy and he always led. I became expert at removing ice screws. If you take out enough protection over a long period of time, you also learn (without knowing it) how to put it in. It's like learning how to cook:

you don't actually have to help your mother get dinner every night to know how, when it's your turn, to get dinner yourself.

I was interested in learning to lead, but the opportunity never came up. We were both just having so much fun the way things were.

One Saturday we decided to climb a lovely route called *Roaring Brook Falls,* which is four pitches. There were Guy, our nephew Dane, another fellow named Ed, and me. Guy was the only one of us who led, and he started up. Suddenly there was a strange rattly, whirring sound. We all quickly looked up, not knowing what to expect, and Ed, who was belaying, got bonked by a large, white, round-faced alarm clock—the type you set on the bedside table at night—which Guy carried in his shirt so as to be sure it would keep going in cold weather. The clock's career as a timepiece ended on the ice at our feet, and Dane intoned, "My, how time flies."

That was the first event.

Guy brought us all up to the belay and took off again. Next, we heard up above a funny scuffling, a sort of yelp, and then, "Oh damn! I've sheered off my crampon points." Our leader improvised and reached the next belay.

That was the second event.

Back in those days we were in love with the romance of climbing. We had read the great masters of Alpine lore—Geoffrey Winthrop Young, Leslie Stephens, Whymper, and Mummery—and would sprinkle their stories into our conversation. One of our favorite lines when we were in a tough place was: "And Vedenz was then sent forward with the rope." Vedenz was, apparently, a guide, or maybe only a porter, who was constantly getting the British gentleman climbers out of trouble.

Now, at this critical moment, with our leader sidelined, I thought, My chance to be Vedenz! Guy thought so too, since he handed me the rack and said it was up to me to lead the last two pitches.

That was the beginning of leading ice for me: the breakthrough. Next came consolidation.

Not long after the *Roaring Brook Falls* incident, we made the even longer drive up to New Hampshire's White Mountains. We wanted to climb the famous Willey Slide, which we knew to be low-angle and not terribly hard (harder then than it is now, though, of course!). Though easy, it has many pitches, and all of those belays are out on the ice, anchored by ice screws: no sturdy trees to quickly throw a sling around.

We were a party of three: Guy, me, and our good friend Lou. Lou didn't lead, so Guy and I agreed we'd flip and put Lou in the middle, which was fine with him.

At the base of the long, wide floe—it looked to me like several acres of perfect ice!—we begin gearing up. Crampons first. Lou and I were crouched, tightening straps, when we became aware of frantic movement next to us. Guy was up to his elbows, burrowing in his pack, pitching things out. Useless gear was strewn in a heap on the snow, disorganized. His eyes were wide. I heard an inarticulate gurgle that sounded like a person strangling. Guy had forgotten his crampons.

That was the third event.

His loss, that day, was my gain. As Lou and I moved steadily up Willey's thick floes, we caught glimpses of Guy, poor thing, pacing up and down the old railroad line that ran through the notch below. He had dwindled to doll size when I finally reached the top.

Those two incidents—the one at Chapel Pond, the other on Willey Slide—completely removed our mental block about my leading. The next time we were in Huntington Ravine, Guy handed *me* the rack and I led *him* up Pinnacle Gully.

At the millennium's turn this tale probably rings pathetic: a woman of limited vision; a man so domineering as to surrender the lead only when physically handicapped. I don't see it that way. To me it tells less about us—remember, I saw almost no other women on the ice at all—and more about the ways of history, the changing vision of expected roles, the slowly evolving perceptions of possibilities. Perhaps the message is in the eye of the beholder.

# THE GEAR-FREAK CAPER

## A STORY

by Rex Slim (with apologies to Woody Allen)

**W**oody Allen's inspired narrative, "The Whore of Mensa," which appeared in *The New Yorker* a quarter century ago, provided the takeoff point for this tale. As climbing and even hiking became increasingly focused on the latest gear, we found ourselves boorishly uninformed and out of touch. Most of the equipment and materials referred to here, brand-new in the 1970s, will sound antediluvian in the twenty-first century. The same is true for some of the names. Rex Slim bears the same relationship to the prolific mystery writer Rex Stout as our Claudius Fox bears to Mr. Stout's protagonist, Nero Wolfe—familiar figures on the literary scene a generation ago, but who reads them today? Thus we stand convicted, on all fronts, of the opposite tendencies from those satirized in this tall tale, concocted by Guy shortly after reading Allen's gem.

**Source:** This much-published piece originally appeared in the April 1976 issue of *Off Belay*. With the focus switched from technical climbing to straightforward backpacking, it later appeared in *New England Outdoors*. With British gear substituted for American, it came out in *Climber and Rambler*. Then a British anthology of climbing humor, Walt Unsworth's *This Climbing Game* (Viking, 1984), picked it up. By our count, this is its fifth printed setting.

▲ ▼ ▲

**In my business you got to be able to spot a meal ticket from a dry hole right off. I** was pretty sure Lady Luck had sent me home a winner when this tweedy gent with a pipe comes through the door marked "CLAUDIUS FOX PRIVATE INVESTIGATOR" and walks up to my desk.

He smelled like money. Trouble too. But that's my bag, isn't it?

"Mr. Fox?" he queried.

"That's what the name says on the door," I countered.

His suit was rumpled and not exactly new, but you could tell he didn't get it off the rack at Korvette's. His shirt was expensive and the tie was as conservative as a baked potato. But what caught my eye was the tie clasp: a thin, small, neatly embossed golden dollar sign. I liked that.

"My name's Godfrey Gearfreak. I need help, and I'm willing to pay for it," he started in, me not objecting to that last part.

"I've never dealt with a private detective before, but I don't want this to get to the police. You see," his eyes fell, "I'm being blackmailed."

I'd heard this story before. Only this one turned out to have a new wrinkle.

I motioned him to a chair and drew paper and pencil from under the flask in the desk drawer. "Tell me all about it," I mused in my most understanding tone.

"My wife and I used to go rock climbing together a lot. We met in a Sierra Club beginners' group. We used to go to Yosemite, Taquitz, vacations in the Tetons, Rainier, the Gunks, everywhere together."

"Sounds nice and healthy," I smiled. "What went wrong?"

He plunged in: "The equipment—all the climbing gear. I found it fascinating; she was bored by it. I got all the latest catalogs—Chouinard, REI, North Face, Sierra Designs, EMS, you name it. I grooved on the Mountain Safety Research newsletters. I had to try all the latest hardware, each new belay plate and seat harness, not to mention all the new tent designs, pack frames, sleeping bags, stoves . . . "

"And your wife didn't like your spending the money?" I put in.

175

"It's not that. We can afford that kind of money." I liked hearing him say that; it gave me a warm feeling in my wallet.

His voice lowered. "She just never took an interest in the equipment. She still wants to go hiking and climbing on weekends. Clambering around on the rocks is all right, I suppose, but there's so much new gear to try out and read about, I don't want to waste all my free time just out there climbing around.

"Christ, Claudius," he blurted, "who wants to sweat out some lousy 5.7 move when you could be looking at and talking about this hot new foam-back material for cagoules that uses a super K coated nylon taffeta with a .050-inch layer of bonded foam and a lining of thin nylon tricot!"

No question, I had to agree with Gearfreak there.

"Well, I found out there's a place in this town where they'll set you up with a girl who knows all about climbing equipment and will talk with you for an hour about any gear you want to talk about—for a price."

He paused, embarrassed. "Go on," I urged.

"I never wanted to get involved. I'm just looking for a quick, stimulating exchange of ideas on all the latest gear—then I want the girl to leave.

"They've got all kinds of girls—some of them know all the latest tents, some can tell you about ropes and their test strength, some are technical ice-climbing specialists." He sighed a crooked, bitter sigh: "It's really satisfying, Claudius, to spend an evening secluded with a girl who really *understands* how baffles are superior to sewn-through seams and can talk intelligently and sympathetically about proper stitching, who appreciates the difference between goose down and duck down, and who isn't afraid to talk openly about foam as a medium for sleeping bags."

"All sounds great," I commented. "What's the prob?"

"Blackmail! I've been arranging these rendezvous for several months. The price was stiff, but it was worth it. Now they're upping the ante—asking for real money—or they'll tell my wife."

His voice dropped to a whisper: "They've even got a photo of me showing a Sticht belay plate to a young girl in lederhosen."

I was intrigued. I'd heard that the boys down at the Vice Squad were working on some big-time racket involving outdoorsy types, but I also knew they weren't getting anywhere on the case. Maybe this was a lead.

"Tell me what you know about this operation." I hunched over the pad.

He demurred. "But will you help me? Will you take the case?"

I looked again at the thin, small, neatly embossed golden dollar-sign tie clasp. "Seventy-five bucks a day plus expenses. And I don't guarantee results. But I've got some hunches I'd like to play."

He looked assured. I had me a client.

After he left, I also had me a packet of notes on all he knew, including the telephone number for his contact. I was ready to make my first move.

▲ ▼ ▲

Going out to a pay phone so the call could not be traced, I plugged in my dime and dialed the seven delectable digits. A husky voice, like Harlow with bronchitis, answered.

I started off briskly: "I understand a fellow could get a little companionable talk on the advantages and disadvantages of different lightweight stoves at this party."

"I'm totally mystified as to what you're talking about, mister," responded the decidedly unmystified voice.

"I have a hundred here to refresh your memory," I growled.

Madam Husky-Voice was suddenly all business. "Do you want to talk heating capacity or weight and volume, honey?"

"The works," I thought it best not to seem cheap.

"That C-note will get you a nice evening with a girl who knows all the stoves and has tried them out in high winds and at different altitudes. She was one of the first to use the MSR."

"Sounds like my ticket," I opined. I gave her a room number at the Belmont and hung up.

▲ ▼ ▲

An hour later I answered the buzzer at this same room number to see a shapely young sheba who was all Miss Outdoors, from the tip of balaclava right down to the toes of her Civettas. In between she filled out her hiking knickers and L. L. Bean sweater like so many well-packed (but just right) stuff sacks.

Her Kelty bulged with odd shapes and sizes of stoves.

"Hi, I'm Bobbi," she cooed sweetly.

"Baby, I don't know how you got by the house dick," I winced as I pulled her into the room. "Anyone can tell you're an equipment nut."

"A five-spot usually keeps them happy," she smiled confidently. Unshouldering her Kelty, she shot a glance around the room. "Would you like to begin by comparing the heating properties of the Optimus IIIB with the newer MSR?"

I parried, "I've heard the MSR's a fabulous heating machine, but won't simmer on low heat like the Optimus." I had to string her along, see what she'd do, see how far she'd go.

"True," she laughed, a hollow, brittle laugh. "But the weight of that old IIIB never appealed to me. And since you have to carry a fuel bottle anyway . . . "

She started in and kept it up, with just an occasional query or rebuttal from me, for fully an hour. Here she was, probably not old enough to buy a set-up at the local bar, but with all the hardened flippancy of the jaded equipment freak. I was amazed. I mean, I've been around, but this was something new.

When she got through explaining how the adapter valves for the new Rich-Moor stoves accommodated several varieties of fuel, I got up, stretched, and, taking two fifties out of my wallet, stuffed them in the outside pocket of her Kelty.

"Say, you're nice," she grinned suddenly. "Would you like to do it again sometime? Or maybe try something a little different . . . a little unusual?"

"What'd you have in mind?" I countered.

"Well, I have a girlfriend you'd like," she purred. "The two of us could come up and talk about cross-country ski wax for a really divine evening. We could even get into . . . " her voice trailed off, but her lips shaped the word, " . . . bindings." She winked.

"I think we might make a deal," I murmured, bluffing. "I'll call you in a day or so," and I ushered her and her Kelty out the door, familiarly patting her D-rings as she passed.

Pay dirt! I knew I had stumbled right into just the mess the Vice Squad was after. I suppressed a snicker. I knew the lieutenant would be climbing walls (5.9) when he found I had beaten him to the quarry again.

▲ ▼ ▲

Before I took the direct route to my prey, though, I thought I ought to do a little advance nosing around through a third party, a certain shady character of my acquaintance, name of Slightly Roddey, who is willing to give me underworld information on occasion in exchange for my not giving the boys downtown certain information about Slightly Roddey.

Slightly was his usual obnoxious and uncooperative self until reminded of the advantages of being on this side of those Sing Sing walls. Then he sung sung.

"The Vice boys haven't got to first base on this one," Slightly told me over a draft in the Shady Deal Café down on lower Filth Street.

"This operation is really big-time and the cover's held up airtight so far. For fifty bills you can spend a couple of hours with a brunette going over the pros and cons of A-frame tents versus the exoskeleton design, reviewing ventilation condensation, tunnel entrances, mosquito netting, zippers, and cook stove holes.

"For just twenty-five, you can get a set-up with a leggy Swedish broad, lighting lanterns and stoves and testing for beryllium and carbon monoxide.

"If you're into technical climbing, you can climb into and out of every seat harness, chest harness, and leg loop in the book with two cuties who can tell you the fall force each one could absorb and will listen sympathetically to all you want to tell them about different hard hats, even including their energy absorption and lateral rigidity. That would cost you seventy-five bucks."

Slightly paused to order another brew.

"Write down this name: Gloria Rucksack. She's the brains and the muscle behind this one, from what I hear."

"What's her background?" I wheedled.

"She's an equipment nut from way back. You know Jack Stephenson's fancy Warmlite tent?"

"The one with the unique condensation-dispelling properties?" I questioned.

"That's the one. Well, Stephenson doesn't know it, but Gloria Rucksack spent a weekend in the pilot model before he did."

I gulped.

"You know Dirty Harry's new sleeping bags at Alpine Designs?" went on Slightly. "She slept in it the first night the baffles were stitched."

"With or without Dirty Harry?" I quipped.

"You want solid info or witty repartee?" Slightly shot back. "She knows them all—Penberthy, Chouinard, the Whittaker brothers. Anyway, the place you want is a little backpacking supply store on the outskirts of town, Northern Alpine Sports. It's a front, of course. The real operation runs out of the back of the store. You'd probably find Gloria there."

▲ ▼ ▲

An hour later, when I walked into Northern Alpine Sports, a young man in Vibrams asked if he could help me.

"I'd like to see a rucksack," I croaked.

"For what purpose?" he inquired.

"Glory-a only knows," I muttered.

"In that case, go right on back." He knowingly waved me down a long hall that led to a door marked "STOCKROOM EMPLOYEES ONLY." I pushed open the door and gingerly stepped in.

Here indeed was Gloria Rucksack's pleasure palace. The place was a perfect set-up. A huge high-ceilinged room, with windows along one side as tall as your grandmother's giraffe. Only no light showed through the heavy maroon velvet floor-to-ceiling curtains, thickly embroidered with gold. The light was supplied by three glittering silver chandeliers suspended from the ornate ceiling. An Oriental carpet large enough to fly in Farouk and all his concubines buried the floor. Victorian décor all the way.

And girls? Wow! A trio of beauties sat on one outsize sofa, provocatively leafing through the pages of REI catalogs. A gorgeous redhead in crimson knickers, who looked like she'd just been poured into her Whillans seat harness like thick strawberry jam, was sorting hexentrics voluptuously on the floor at one end. Slouched in an armchair near the door, a slender, pretty girl no more that seventeen years old was opening and closing Jumars and Gibbs ascenders.

Within seconds after I entered, a slinky black girl sidled up to me from nowhere, slipping her slim hips in and out of a wraparound pack frame, and breathed huskily, "Would you like to go upstairs and talk about different kinds of back bands?"

"Catch you later at Camp Four, baby," I snapped out of the corner of my mouth. "I got other things on my mind right now."

A honey blond in a leopard-skin 60-40 whispered at me from the other side. "If you're into technical ice, we could have a cozy chat about the test strengths of Salewa tubulars versus wart hogs. And I have a new wrinkle on how to use a Terrordactyl that would tickle you."

Before I could answer, a familiar husky tone from behind me intervened: "Later, Birgit. This one's for me."

Swinging around, I saw before me the queen mama of them all—a statuesque raven-haired Venus who would make anyone forget to button down his supergaiters. Her skirt was like a good tent fly—form-fitted and not too long. And the blouse material was strictly sewn-through.

"You look like you could use a sociable brew in the back room, honey," she purred as she guided me toward a low door near the back, just past a carved-ebony bookcase sporting titles like *Freedom of the Hills, Advanced Rockcraft,* early Chouinard catalogs, and a handsome leather-bound complete set of MSR newsletters.

She slipped a key chain out of her bosom and sorted through the Swiss Army knife, Taylor pocket altimeter, and Dwyer wind meter until she came to a tiny key for the little door. But not before I noticed on that key chain one other little trinket . . . a thin, small, neatly embossed golden dollar sign.

I followed her into a richly appointed little boudoir, and as she walked ahead of me, I said, "Nice little pad you have here, Gloria Rucksack—or should I say . . . Mrs. Gearfreak!"

She wheeled around, sporting a new piece of equipment—a shiny little black revolver that I knew she hadn't picked up at Holubar's. "That's right, Fox, you walked yourself right into the middle of more than you bargained for this time."

"I don't get it, baby," I sauntered, stalling and trying to look calm. "Your old man said he couldn't get you to talk about clevis pins at breakfast."

"That creep?" she snarled. "He doesn't know his rear end from a cook stove hole. What he doesn't know about equipment would fill three Bauer catalogs. Just as soon as I get this operation a little more profitable, it'll be goodbye, Godfrey! And meanwhile, Foxie, you're going to take a little hike of your own—down the middle of the Hudson River in a pair of cement P.A.'s."

I thought fast—and acted faster. With one swift karate chop, I separated Miss Gloria-locks from her shiny black plaything, and in another motion I swooped an extra-large down mummy bag over her head. She ripped out her Swiss Army knife and cut her way out, filling the room with more feathers that you'll see at a Northern Goose Hoedown on Hudson Bay. By this time, though, Your Humble Narrator had the revolver and the outing was over.

The rest of the story came out downtown, and today Miss Rucksack—Mrs. Gearfreak—is doing a ten-year bivouac in a really windproof stand-up tent at Sing Sing.

Except for my check from Mr. Godfrey Gearfreak, which arrived in the mail, I neither saw nor heard from him again. But I've been told that he now roams the High Sierra, with no climbing hardware, no tent, and just an old army blanket in which he rolls all his simple belongings, so that he needs no fancy pack. They say he takes no interest in the latest gadgets and gear of the other climbers and hikers he meets on the trail, but simply invites them to join him in looking at the birds and the wildflowers.

# FIVE WINTER TRIPS

## THE END OF ADVENTURE?

Roderick Nash, intellectual guru of the "wilderness and the American mind," has warned, "The future of American wilderness depends on American civilization's deliberately keeping it wild."

This obvious irony is all too true. Over the three decades we have been climbing, we have watched a steady erosion of wildness, a dispiriting dilution of the terms of adventure available in the mountains we knew. It's been going on everywhere in the world. This tale of five different winter trips, each attempting the same itinerary—originally all too challenging, now all too easy—tries to encapsulate what to us is nothing short of a tragic loss.

Winter in the mountains, any mountains, almost guarantees a wild adventure. Even our runty little New England hills boast winter weather that makes them savage antagonists to the aspiring winter climber. They serve as splendid arena for adventure.

Yet, in the name of safety or democracy, we have bureaucrats and hovering meddlers who would soften the blow; muffle the mountain gods, deprive the winter climber of the opportunity for genuine adventure. They would establish havens of safety at close intervals in the mountains, intrude communication and access into the remoter fastness, refine search-and-rescue capability in an uncontestable campaign to save human life. For the highest of motives, they would emasculate the wilderness experience.

**Source:** *Wilderness Ethics.*

▲ ▼ ▲

**A very real issue confronting the future of mountain recreation is whether we are** going to reduce the winter mountain experience to accommodate our limited powers and limited vision, or whether we are going to take it on the mountain's terms and rise to the challenge.

Five stories of winter mountaineering adventure illustrate the changing conditions of winter climbing. Taken sequentially, they illustrate the progressive degradation of the mountain spirit when humanity imposes its own terms on nature.

### Trip 1

In 1962 the first known attempt to traverse the White Mountains in winter was launched. Back then, climbing the Northeast's mountains in winter was tough. Very few people came to the winter mountains. Parties needed to break out on snowshoes nearly every trail they used. Some peaks with trails built after 1970 were trailless before then. The Kancamagus Highway, which slices through the mountains from east to west, was not plowed, making many peaks in the interior far less accessible.

Then, safety was the watchword. Because of the remoteness and inherent danger, these early-winter climbers loaded themselves down with gear enough to confront any emergency, slouching cumbrously about in large parties. Consequently, they traveled very slowly. As one authoritative winter climber of the day stressed, "Safety must prevail over speed."

Inevitably, under all this weight and with the odds stacked so heavily against them, winter climbers set very limited objectives. Within those limits, that generation accomplished some impressive feats. Despite an underlying and perhaps inhibiting conservative approach, their boldness and love of adventure would not be suppressed.

In 1962 Robert Collin conceived the plan of traversing the White Mountains in winter. Collin was a winter trip leader who had learned and taught in the winter programs of both the Adirondack Mountain Club and Appalachian Mountain Club. He had written state-of-the-art articles on winter backpacking. He was the acknowledged authority. The route he proposed would take his party past all of the Appalachian Mountain Club's high mountain huts, covering roughly fifty-five miles.

The demands of that trip in 1962 are difficult to envision today. Now two of those huts are kept open all winter, furnished with an efficient woodstove, and staffed by a caretaker. Then they were all closed and cold, no haven for the winter traveler.

In point of fact, there were times in the early days when the huts were left unlocked, but they remained unheated, and a big, cold building is a doubtful asset in winter. You win protection from storm and insulation from snow, but you lose the cozy heat-retaining confines of a small tent. The coldest night we have ever spent in the "outdoors" was "indoors" at one of the AMC huts back in those days when they were left unlocked: Lincoln's Birthday in 1967, when the summit of Mount Washington reported forty-one degrees below zero, the top of Cannon thirty-six degrees below zero, and we were higher than Cannon, across the valley at Greenleaf Hut. We are not at all sure it was an advantage to sleep on the open floor of the cavernous, drafty hut, its wood floors creaking and snapping all night in the extreme cold. Probably we'd have been warmer in a tent, where our body heat would not have been dissipated fruitlessly. So whether Collin's party had access to the huts or not makes little difference: they were of little value compared with the two that are open (and heated) today.

Furthermore, Crawford Notch, the halfway point of Collin's proposed trip, was without shelter of any kind. In those days a summer resort, the Crawford House, sprawled its elegant finery over the manicured lawns of the notch, but in winter all that luxury was boarded up tight. Wind sighed and whistled through the lifeless notch, in the same way it had when an 1850s traveler noted:

*For two-thirds of the year a more desolate place can hardly be imagined than this Notch. Dismal winds moan through the leafless trees, and through the fissures of the rocks . . . Woe, then, to poor mortality, when the snow falls*

*fast, and the king of tempest rides on the wings of the hurricane through the*
*clouds, armed with winter's cold, blinding sleet, and avalanches of ice!*

⚜ ▽ ⚜

Between the huts, the trails (then much less carefully blazed) saw essentially
no traffic. None. Zero. That meant Collin's party would have to break out every
trail every day and not waste too much time by losing and refinding the trail.
The physical demands of constant trailbreaking and the steady pressures of
trying to discern where the trail went was a trial few experience today.

Worse than the physical toll was the psychological burden of knowing
they were the only folks out there. No help was at hand. Rescue techniques
were primitive, but that wasn't important, because the main thing was that
rescue was not likely to happen. The climbers were strictly on their own.
This is a psychological burden that few experience today. The average winter climber of the 1990s may occasionally break out a new trail and can
understand how tough it would have been to break trail every day. But winter
climbers today, amid such a healthy population of other winter recreationists,
cannot appreciate the psychological burden of being out there . . .
all . . . by . . . yourself . . .

Collin proposed that his group traverse from west to east, ending their
trip with crossing the Presidentials. They would be out for nine days, carrying all their food and gear, camping out each night. This meant toughing it
out for the long slog up and over the Franconias and the humpy ridge to
Garfield, across the Twin Range and Bonds in the remote Pemigewasset
wilderness, through the Zealand Valley and out to Crawford Notch. And after
that, a full winter Presidentials traverse, plus a jaunt up to Carter Notch.

If you just put your head down and doggedly kept placing one snowshoe
in front of the other; if you could stand the hardship of your gear getting
soggier and soggier, your down sleeping bag becoming less comfortable and
certainly less effective as it picked up more and more moisture; if you could
put up with little annoyances like constantly hitting snowy branches overhead with your overloaded pack, thus dumping snow on your head and
shoulders and down between your back and your pack (in which warm spot
it immediately turned to moisture and wetted further into your clothing); if
you could stand the hardship of tenting out every night—then you could walk
from Franconia Notch to Crawford Notch in winter. As Collin said in one of

his articles, "If you insist on being comfortable at all times you had better stay home."

The Collin party did put their heads down and reach Crawford Notch, but here they met defeat. The Presidentials' famous winter winds can ruin the plans of even the most determined climbers. Collin and his group were beaten back by relentless high winds and blowing snow of that above-tree-line world and were forced to retreat. After an already grueling struggle to travel from Franconia Notch to Crawford Notch, they simply had no further resources to wait out a break in the weather. They had "lost."

Mountains 1, Hikers 0.

But what they had won was remarkable. Even though they failed in their ultimate objective, their "failure" was more notable than the success that occurred nearly twenty years later. Collin was out there when climbers took the mountains on their own rough and deliberate terms. He and his group were always breaking and finding the winter trail, often obscured in deep snow. Perhaps hardest of all, they carried the psychological burden of their isolation. A lot has changed in forty years!

### Trip 2

In the winter of 1968–1969 came a second attempt. By this time the so-called backpacking boom had begun but had little affected the winter hiking population. As one measure, only about a dozen individuals had climbed all of the four-thousand-footers of either the White Mountains or Adirondacks in winter (compared with hundreds today), and no one had done both in the snowy season. Most trails remained untouched all winter long, the snow accumulating to great depth without the compaction of passing snowshoers or cross-country skiers.

The year 1969 broke all records for depth of snow in New Hampshire. November 1968's snowfall as measured on the summit of Mount Washington was already 87 inches. December added another whopping 104 inches to the pile. Those records continue to stand, as does the record set in February 1969 of 173 inches. In all, that amazing winter, the total snowfall accumulation reached very nearly fifty feet! On the trails that led to and connected the AMC huts, an almost incredible depth of soft snow was building up as early as November.

A party of four chose to deploy their resources in a new way so as to facilitate the winter traverse: one pair would start from Lonesome Lake, the westward extremity of the mountains, and work eastward toward the Presidentials. The other pair would start at the Presidentials, do a standard Presidentials traverse, and then keep going. The two parties would meet roughly halfway. From then on the going would be easier because the trails would be packed. Or such was the elegantly worked-out theory.

On December 24, 1968, the first pair, Dave Ingalls and Roy Kligfield, started from Franconia Notch. With huge packs laden for the lengthy journey, they snowshoed up to tree line on the Franconia Ridge, crossed over the alpine zone and Mount Lafayette, and camped at Garfield Pond on that first night. Bitter cold temperatures and high winds greeted their efforts next morning, but they laboriously chugged on over Garfield and the ups and downs of that ridge, reaching Galehead Hut for a cold Christmas night. Ingalls had partially frozen a few toes the year before, and that night he noted ominous signs of recurring frostbite. Still determined, they took off from Galehead Hut and climbed South Twin. On the high wind-racked ridge beyond South Twin, the snow had drifted so deep among the stunted trees that it was hopeless to find the trail. Repeatedly they sunk in "spruce traps" and had to struggle out of their enormous packs to extricate themselves. Ingalls realized his feet had lost all feeling. In desperation they opted to return to the lower and more sheltered elevation of Galehead Hut, where the temperature that night sunk to minus twenty-four degrees.

The next morning, December 27, the two climbers began a desperate flight for survival. They headed down and out, constantly losing and refinding the trail along the Gale River, physically worn and defeated, and with the certain knowledge that Ingalls's feet were in bad shape. By late afternoon they slid down the last snow bank to the plowed road. They didn't hitch a ride; they walked out in front of the next car and forced it to stop. Ingalls elected to be driven to Massachusetts General Hospital in hopes of more knowledgeable medical care there than at any north country hospital. After a long recuperation, he walked back into the world with several toes lost forever, a victim of frostbite.

The other pair consisted of one of the authors, Guy, and his then sixteen-year-old son Johnny. An earlier story in this collection, "Winter Above Tree Line," tells the story of their attempt—just as fruitless on their end as the Ingalls-Kligfield fiasco.

Mountains 2, Hikers 0.

The second attempt to traverse the White Mountains in winter was over. All four of us were totally and humiliatingly defeated. Dave Ingalls had lost toes. The raw power, the malign destructive force of a mountain winter, had fully impressed us.

## Trip 3

In 1977 an ill-fated third attempt began.

By this time the ground rules had begun to change. Some of nature's advantage was neutralized. That is, the Appalachian Mountain Club had opened two of its high huts to wintertime use, installing a woodstove and a full-time caretaker at both Zealand Falls and Carter Notch. The volume of winter climbing had greatly increased, a fact that implied that many trails were now regularly broken out. Still, the real boom in winter climbing lay ahead in the 1980s, and many trails remained little used.

Again Guy was involved, this time opting for the adventure of a slow attempt. His story follows.

▲ ▼ ▲

Going as spartan as I dared, I still had a monstrously heavy pack, but the snows, while deep that year, did not reach the absurd depths of 1968–1969.

The first day, February 3, after a quick packless ascent to Lonesome Lake and back, I climbed Mount Lafayette, finding a welcome packed-out trail to tree line. After I crossed the alpine zone of Lafayette in moderately high winds, I plunged down into the Garfield Ridge and found that no one had been there before me that winter. That trail was not as well maintained then as now. Repeatedly I lost and refound the trail. Within a short time I was exhausted, and I set up camp as a light snowfall began.

By morning fresh snow lay deep on the old surface and trees were drenched in new powder. On and off the trail I battled my heavy pack through the snow-laden forest, getting soaking wet in the process. Because of the energy required, I could keep warm in just a wool net undershirt and a 60-40 parka (the uniform of the 1970s winter climber), thus was able to reserve my wool shirt and sweater for warmth in camp. Still, I was able to go only about five miles: in those days of unpacked trails, many of us found that about five miles was a fairly standard maximum distance for a full day's vigorous effort. I camped again along the trail, a half mile short of Galehead Hut.

That night I noted my sleeping bag was getting damp and beginning to lose heating value. The parka and windpants, along with the net undershirt, were of course soaked through from the perpetual contact with snowy trees. I had a change of undershirt and dry wool shirt and sweater to wear in the tent. But if I were to have dry things for the next night, I had to be prepared to put the wet things back on in the morning. How to keep them from freezing solid? The parka and windpants I spread between the two foam pads I was sleeping on, so my body heat would keep them flexible. The net undershirt came into the sleeping bag with me: there it would dry out overnight, but of course its moisture would be transferred to the sleeping bag, further reducing its effectiveness.

On the next day I struggled up to Galehead Hut and South Twin. Along the ridge beyond I repeatedly lost trail and refound it. Even when I was on the trail I had to push through snow-laden branches all day long.

I noticed an interesting phenomenon. When I lost the trail, I would zig-zag across the ridge, casting about to find it. Amid the dense scrub of the Twin Range, carrying a week's backpack, this was an utterly exhausting procedure. The compaction of the snow amid the conifers was completely unpredictable, randomly ranging from firm to plunging in up to my waist, with the not-infrequent surprise of plunging nearly to ground level, with six or eight feet of soft snow and interlaced evergreen branches as my sudden neighbors. As I battled with this frustrating environment, I would push, push, push to keep fighting through the trees, looking for the trail. Sometimes I'd spend as much as a full hour off-trail, making little progress. When I'd finally and unmistakably come across the trail, my mind would say, OK, you've lost time; now that you've got open sailing, make it up—full speed ahead! But my body, after unrelenting push, push, push through the spruce traps, would rebel. All of a sudden, though mentally thinking full speed ahead, I'd find myself achingly weary and lethargic, ready to rest.

Another five miles that day—with more physical strain than twenty-five miles in summer—brought me, at almost dusk, to the first sign of other human activity that winter since I had left Mount Lafayette more that fifty hours earlier: fresh snowshoe tracks just east of the top of Mount Zealand. I collapsed on them and immediately set up camp. My clothes were soaked from the contact with snow all day. The sleeping bag was now also distinctly clammy.

On the fourth day out, I followed the packed-out trail with unalloyed gratitude until I reached Zealand Falls Hut by late morning. Outside the hut, as I arrived in my encrusted parka and windpants, I met a nattily attired cross-country skier just placing his dainty boots in his bindings, the first fellow human I'd seen in about seventy-two hours. When I couldn't resist mentioning the fact, it brought no response. I had the impression that the idea of crossing the mountains alone for three days was so remote from the possibilities of his world (let alone the desirabilities) that he simply didn't take it in. I've since learned not to bring up my itineraries with those to whom they would only seem bizarre and certainly not sensible.

With my clothing and sleeping bag desperately wet, I surrendered to the availability of this island of fellow humanity's conveniences and spent three hours at the hut attempting to dry out enough to survive one more night out. Then I continued on my way to reach the Ethan Pond area for my fourth night out. The pond proved a windy place, the temperature below zero, and my bag by no means completely dry. It was a shivery night.

The next day I stumbled down to Crawford Notch. There I fled for my car and home (and Laura). To have superimposed a Presidentials traverse on the exhausting trip I'd just completed was not to be thought of.

Mountains 3, Hikers 0.

It was a shrunken victory to have crossed from Franconia to Crawford Notch by myself in winter. The victory was cheapened by the use of the hut to dry out partially. And, of course, the big prize of also crossing the Presidentials had been far beyond my reach.

### Trip 4

In 1980 a party of three, the two of us plus our good friend Mike (mentioned in "Education in Verticality: A Short Comedy or Farce in Four Scenes," the Interlude between parts one and two), set off to accomplish that winter traverse of the White Mountains. Remember: it was still the Last Great Problem, not yet accomplished.

But now a lot of the rules of the game had changed. Two of the Appalachian Mountain Club's high mountain huts were open in winter, provided with a warm stove and staffed by a caretaker. Also, in that formerly wild and lonely waste of Crawford Notch, a cheerful AMC roadside hostel now glowed warm all winter, welcoming all winter visitors. Even more significant, the winter climbing boom was well under way. Snowshoers and skiers were starting to fan out all over the more popular trails. The taming of the mountains in winter was well advanced.

Of course your humble heroes were hard-line purists, and so was our friend Mike. No indoor sleeping for us! No cheery stove or caretaker's care for us! We would carry our tent, a heavy three-person model, and camp in it every night. This would be our way of protesting the belittling of winter adventure that we saw represented by the opening of comfortable backcountry facilities in winter.

As in 1969, weather played a vital role in the outcome. The winter of 1979–1980 was snowless, something unprecedented in our lifetimes. It meant very fast travel, sometimes faster than in summer. Most trails were a sheet of ice, like a frozen sidewalk. That meant strapping on crampons for the whole day and striding along almost like in summer. Deep snow was not obscuring the trailway, so trail finding was no problem whatsoever.

For our trio it meant fast going, which meant fewer days out, which meant lighter loads. With no snow, we didn't have to carry snowshoes, didn't have to laboriously break trail, didn't even have to find the trail. No snow would be knocked off branches by high packs to soak into clothing. Success seemed assured.

On day one we ran up to the hut at Lonesome Lake without packs, tagged it, and jogged down to the road again, then picked up our loads and started out. One hut down, seven to go.

It was a warm, overcast day with a forecast of rain, that dreaded scourge of winter mountain travelers. Before we'd reached Greenleaf Hut (number two) it began to drizzle. As we put on rain gear, we heard the wind picking up out of the south—a bad sign. We knew it would be a bit of a tussle to get over Mount Lafayette with its above-tree-line exposure. It was.

The lightest member of our party was carrying a frame pack (well laden), and that pack acted like a sail, picking her up and setting her down rather roughly and not on her feet. Her biggest companion, Mike, would hoist her up by the top bar of the frame—equivalent to the scruff of the neck—stick a piece of chocolate in her mouth (for energy and morale), and we'd struggle on. After an hour's walking in something akin to the combined rinse and spin cycles of a washing machine, we reached the windblown and rain-pelted summit of Lafayette, then continued on across to North Lafayette and down into the shelter of the trees. Blessed trees! We still got wetter, but now we were out of that wind.

Wet: we know of no rain gear made that can stand up to the punishment of wind-driven rain. We were soaked. At first we hoped to camp on Garfield Pond, but there we found half a foot of standing water. We resolved to press on through the dusk to shelter on the other side of Garfield. So much for purity! Well, we said, we'll camp out on all the other nights; we'll use the shelter just this first night to try to get dry.

The next morning we made an assessment. We were thoroughly soaked and highly vulnerable to any drop in temperature. In the old days, we simply could not have continued in our dampened state. We would unquestionably have aborted the trip. But in 1980 we knew that Zealand Falls Hut was open. Well, we decided, after we get really dry at Zealand, then we'll be set and we'll use the tent every night and not go near those heated buildings. So on day two we slogged all the way to Zealand, tagging Galehead Hut (number three) on the way and making the last stream crossing in the dark. By the stove at Zealand, we felt warmth oozing in—and the adventure oozing away.

Well, funny thing: next morning we still felt damp in vital spots, especially the sleeping bags. Also, our feet were sore from walking in inflexible crampons for two dawn-to-after-dark days. So we decided to make our third day a short one—sort of a rest day—and just go as far as Crawford Notch. Here we would finish the drying process at the hostel and rest up. This final drying should put us in excellent shape for tackling the Presidentials.

On day four, thoroughly dry at last, we marched up the Crawford Path to Mizpah Hut (number five). On we crunched over the Southern Presidentials. Things were getting exciting again. We were in the land above the trees, where anything can happen. We reached Lakes of the Clouds Hut (number six) about 2:30 P.M. Time for discussion: we could go on and camp someplace just on the other side of Washington, like Sphinx Col. Or . . . we could stay in the basement room at the hut that is kept open by the Appalachian Mountain Club for winter backpackers. This basement refuge is not the Ritz: known to climbers as "the Dungeon," it is damp and dark, about three-quarters of the space taken up by two plywood sheets, one over the other, forming sleeping platforms. But the Dungeon has one distinct advantage: it is proof against the notorious Presidentials wind. When your ethics have been thoroughly eroded, it gets easier to give in to temptation.

The next day we were walking by 7 A.M. It was cloudy and blowy, but not too cold, a manageable day for the job, which was to cross the Presidentials. We were over four lofty summits and down to Madison Springs Hut (the second-to-last hut: number seven) by a few minutes after noon. The plan was to camp someplace in the Great Gulf below—finally to use that heavy tent. But as we hurried down Madison Gulf Trail, we felt it was still too early to camp. As we kept walking, it came into our heads that we had a chance of getting to Carter Notch Hut (number eight and last!) that night. What a day *that* would be—to walk from Lakes of the Clouds Hut to Carter Notch Hut via Madison in one winter day! We also had in mind that the welcome there would be warm: the winter caretaker, Peter Crane, had promised to bake a celebratory cake! We knew it would be past dark when we got to Carter, but, then, the sight of that hut and Peter's smiling face would be all the sweeter.

So that heavy tent never came out of the stuff sack.

Mountains 3, Hikers 1.

But a victory? Not really. Maybe we should stop keeping score. We don't think of a successful climb as defeating a mountain—on the contrary, it celebrates that mountain.

More important, it was perfectly obvious that our "success" was based completely on the shelter of five buildings, three of them heated. Had we not had warm stoves at Zealand and Crawford, we would have beaten a retreat after getting so wet the first day. We had definitely not taken nature on her own terms. We had simply passed quickly through the natural world to go from building to building.

**Trip 5**

In 1989 the final chapter in the sequence of five winter mountain trips was recorded. By now the rules of the game had changed still more. Now winter climbing was a popular sport; both snowshoes and skis crossed and recrossed all major trails all winter long. The two AMC huts were open, Crawford was a well-lit and well-heated oasis, and the surrounding areas were well populated. By now, too, the Randolph Mountain Club paid a caretaker to live in and supervise guests at Greyknob, a cozy cabin high on the flanks of Adams in the Northern Presidentials.

We decided to demonstrate graphically just how the terms of the mountain traverse had changed. Early in the winter, Guy visited both the RMC's Greyknob and AMC's Zealand Falls Hut, talked with the caretakers, and secured permission to leave a small cache of food, mouseproof in a metal container, at each place. Cheating? Sure. But that was the point: to demonstrate how the open facilities, well-packed trails, and crowds of people had completely changed the wilderness experience since Collin's day and even our own previous efforts of 1968 and 1977.

⚬ ▾ ⚬

On the morning of February 9, I snowshoed up the 1.6-mile packed trail to Lonesome Lake and touched the AMC hut. I carried only a small day pack containing a sleeping bag, a small supply of extra clothes, two lunches, and a few supper items, which would not need cooking. I went very light on first-aid supplies, but had parachute cord, tape, and a knife in case of needing to patch snowshoes. Total pack weight: twenty-seven pounds. When I came back down to the road and started up Lafayette I encountered five or six other parties climbing Lafayette. It was below zero and blowing hard, so only one other party went to the top, as far as I knew. From there I turned north into the gale and began the traverse toward Garfield and the Twin Range. By the time I reached tree line on the Garfield Ridge, I was glad enough to escape the punishment of the wind. Trying to be sure not to get dehydrated, I kept sipping water from my one canteen, secure in the knowledge that a vigorous stream flowed near the Garfield Ridge tent site shelter, a water supply I had often used in winter and never found frozen solid.

On the top of Mount Garfield I drained the last of my water and dropped down to the shelter in the last daylight. Consternation! And worse! That reliable stream *was* dry this particular winter. It had been a dry fall and late snow cover; the meager groundwater had simply frozen shut before the insulating snow cover came. When I dug down through the now ample snow all the way to the ground, I found but dry stones. It was getting dark, still windy, I had no tent, and thus was reasonably committed to staying the night in the shelter.

So I stuffed my canteen completely full of snow and took it in the sleeping bag with me. I ate a completely dry supper that night, well aware of the dangers of dehydration in winter, with almost fifty miles yet to traverse. In the morning my canteen had melted barely enough water to dampen a bit of cereal. Then I packed up and snowshoed two waterless miles to a side trail that I knew reached a substantial stream, the Gale River, in just under a mile. I'd lose a lot of elevation and would have to come back up, but I simply had to have water. At the river I drank and drank, my body soaking it in with little apparent effect. Then I filled a full quart and climbed back up to my trail and continued on my way. That night, after eleven and a half miles and a lot of climbing, I reached Zealand Falls Hut.

Here was warmth, a crowd of people, the friendly caretakers—and my cache of food. I spent two nights here, soaking in the heat, water, and hot food, and spending the day between on a lighthearted bushwhack romp with the caretakers and Kita, their energetic canine friend.

On the next morning, again carrying two lunches and one cold dinner, I started early, crossed the Willey Range, and was down for a morning cup of cocoa with yet another friendly caretaker at Crawford Notch. Then I climbed to tree line on the Presidentials.

Now came the only real question: would the infamous Presidentials weather suffer me to cross unharmed? The temperature was moderately cold and the winds reasonably stiff, but both were manageable. As I passed above forty-four hundred feet or so, however, I encountered dense cloud, light blowing snow, and very low visibility. Crossing the heights of Mount Monroe, I was barely able to keep cairns in view. In that whiteout, each projecting rime-covered rock could be mistaken for a cairn. I inched across, with that sense of being right on the edge of losing contact with where I was. Finally I recognized the summit rocks of Monroe and began the slow, difficult process of locating each cairn on the descent route, while also coping with its steepness and an alarming tendency of the snow to form wind-slab over the old hard-frozen surface—a recipe for mini-avalanches, which I had to be absolutely sure not to start. (To slide on that steep slope would have afforded enough speed to make collision with boulders somewhere in the whiteout below a most undesirable event, especially with no companions.) Eventually the surface leveled out, and finally, a few feet away, the side of AMC's Lakes of the Clouds Hut loomed in the cloud.

After a night in the Dungeon, I set out in high winds and continued low visibility toward Mount Washington. It was desperately slow going for a while, but suddenly the clouds cleaved completely, and visibility went from fifty feet to fifty miles in a few seconds. Looking back, I could clearly see the Franconia Ridge on the horizon, from whence I had come during the previous four days. Within minutes all the cloud was gone from Washington as well, and the summit buildings emerged clear against the deep blue sky. I half ran, half stumbled upward with delight, my feet warming with the exercise.

On the top of Mount Washington—on top of the world, I felt, at least my world of winter adventure in the Northeast—yet another form of cheating was available. Normally the Mount Washington Observatory makes it an absolute rule that there is no refuge for winter hikers on top. If they did not, they would be plagued with a multitude of visitors, many of them poorly equipped and more or less counting on help at the top. But, by coincidence, Peter Crane, our host at Carter Notch in 1980, now happened to be working at the observatory that winter and had invited us to stop in for tea sometime. This I now did—in fact, I drank several cups of cocoa and filled my empty canteen with water. (We emphasize that this is not a generally available option; it is proper that winter hikers should be on their own resources completely on Mount Washington. Remember: part of the point of this trip was to be cheating.)

In high winds and cold, but with splendid visibility, I continued on across the Presidentials, climbing both Jefferson and Adams before dropping down the north flank of Adams to Greyknob and my next cache. Here was another sociable night with yet another friendly caretaker.

During the night the winds continued and the temperature dropped. I wondered, as morning approached, if the weather gods would permit me to climb once more into their realm, to cross over the range, touch the seventh hut at Madison Col, and descend the other side toward the eighth and final hut at Carter? In the event, although the temperature was fourteen below zero, and winds were measured up to eighty-five miles per hour at the Mount Washington Observatory that morning, I had the wind largely at my back and, after the first half mile, also could put mountain mass between me and that dreadful wind. So I did make it across. Once down in the trees it was a shoo-in to the valley, my last cache of food (hidden in the woods at roadside), and up the easy 3.8-mile trail to Carter Hut.

Success? Well, yes. I crossed the mountains in winter with a twenty-seven-pound pack. But what did I personally achieve? Nothing terribly impressive. The feat was easily accomplished because I had so much help:

open buildings for overnight shelter all the way, heat in some of them, friendly caretakers to visit, packed trails every foot of the way, plenty of other people around (at times). Most important was the psychological security of people, facilities, technology, escorting me all the way. It was not a wilderness experience. There were exciting moments; there were difficulties; there were times when I definitely had to think hard and work hard to ensure my own safety and success. But in no way was I strictly forced to rely on my own resources alone. I had help and support all around.

In every sense of the word, Bob Collin's "failure" of 1962 was more impressive than my "success" of 1989, just as our three-person party's "success" of 1980 had been less of an adventure, less of an accomplishment, than that desperate struggle four of us had in 1968 and one had in 1977.

Wildness is such a small thing in the Northeast. A very little tampering with it causes frightful ripples. You don't *have* to stay in the heated huts. Of course, we don't. But the mere fact that they are there changes the experience forever. One cannot ignore their presence. If they are there, one can never do what Collin attempted. One can never enter the woods and say, Now I am truly on my own. That bail-out retreat is always in the back of one's mind.

On a global scale, the physical proportions are different, but the essential equation can be reduced to the same stark prospect. The trivialization of Mount Everest—and that mountain's ominous response—is where the line is etched sharpest.

It is a subtle thing: the maintenance of the illusion of wildness. The line is very finely drawn. The game—and it is nothing but a game—is delicately played. If we want our wildness, we must work for it. Decide where we want the line and hold it there.

But the erosion is so creeping. It is like the tide coming in, first a foot from your toes, then up to your knees, and in a short while over your head. You never saw it move, but you are drowning and there is no more wildness.

The environmentalist Jack Turner has warned, "We lost the wild bit by bit for ten thousand years, and forgave each loss and then forgot. Now we face the final loss."

# WHY THE LORAX LOST

**T**hroughout our years as climbers, we always figured climbers were children at heart. Every once in a while, we'd encounter a climber who didn't seem to fit in with the rest of us, who lacked that humor and spark and love of the zany and absurd. We finally figured out their trouble: they were the grown-ups. Of course they didn't feel comfortable in the childlike world of climbing.

So it's not surprising that climbers enjoy children's literature. A few years ago Dr. Seuss's inspired creation *The Lorax* was especially popular among climbers and outdoors people of all sorts.

But we had a disturbing feeling that the full lessons of *The Lorax* were going unheeded. So we wrote the following essay in an attempt to stir thinking that might go beyond the simplistic politics and fallacious economics of early environmentalism. Most of the stories in this collection are meant simply to entertain. But we hope a few messages are transmitted, not least in this closing story.

**Source:** Adapted from *Wilderness Ethics.*

▲ ▼ ▲

**Logging companies in the Northwest have protested little children reading Dr. Seuss's** *The Lorax* in public schools. Sinister propaganda has been detected in the singsong make-believe doggerel of that modern-day Chaucer of children's literature.

The loggers know the enemy well. *The Lorax* is indeed a threat to their way of life, if the latter be defined as a relentless exploitation of limited resources in pursuit of nonsustainable markets.

If you do not know this particular gem of Seussiana, you should. Get it; read it; take heed.

But when you do, pay close attention. There is more in *The Lorax* than either its more ardent fans or its vociferous critics have noticed, we suspect. It is, the logging censors notwithstanding, definitely not a one-sided view of reality. Dr. Seuss has a sermon for the conservationist as well as for the exploiters.

Consider, for example, who wins. Well, nobody really, and certainly not the Lorax. And, as in any good Greek or Shakespearean tragedy, it's his own fault. That makes it no less a tragedy; indeed, is it not an essential element of high tragedy that Lear, Othello, Oedipus, and Antigone bring on their own fate? So too does the tragicomic figure of the Lorax, in a way. But that only makes the story more realistic, and sad, and relevant to all of us.

If you have not read *The Lorax,* you should be aware that no prose synopsis can do justice to Dr. Seuss's inspired nonsense-sense. Nor should you miss the illustrations. Be sure to get a copy of the original, then come back and read this chapter again. Meanwhile, we'll try to keep you with us for now.

The obvious villain of the piece is the Once-ler, who destroys the beautiful forest of Truffala trees to supply a fast-growth market for Thneeds, a trivial product that people buy in large quantities until the last Truffala Tree is cut. In the process of exploiting the forest of Truffala Trees, the Once-ler destroys the habitat of the forest creatures and pollutes the waters therein. The raw material depleted, the market collapses, and the Once-ler is left to live in a depressed area.

You can easily see that the Once-ler and his one-shot exploitative methods are the target of Dr. Seuss. Those Northwest loggers sure saw it that way. In truth, the poem is a searing indictment of cut-and-run logging, of the heedless pollution of waters, of the destruction of wildlife habitat, and of the failure to think about the future and to understand the conditions for continued economic development. Dr. Seuss exposes the fallacy of "biggering"; the horrors of Gluppity-Glupp, and also Schloppity-Schlopp; the environmental impact of Brown Bar-ba-loots, Swomee-Swans, and Humming-Fish; and the ultimate disaster resulting from one-shot exploitation and the depletion of this earth's Truffalian natural heritage.

But look at some of the other targets that Dr. Seuss's nonsense strikes. Who buys Thneeds? The Lorax perceives little marginal utility for this product, and consequently projects poor sales. But the Once-ler has done his market research. When the first customer comes along, he "happily" buys the first Thneed (at $3.98), and from then on Thneeds are a growth industry.

The entire chain of tragic consequences unleashed by the Once-ler and his production methods would never have occurred had not a sizable proportion of the public "happily" accepted Thneeds as a part of their way of life. There could be no Once-ler without a thoughtless public that adopted Thneeds as a necessity of modern living. Or, better yet, the Once-ler would have sought to produce something else, perhaps something that left undisturbed the Truffala Trees and their associated water and wildlife. In the economist George Stigler's felicitous phrase, blaming the producers of frivolous products for the squandering of resources is like blaming waiters for obesity.

Are the eager fans of *The Lorax* listening? Is it the producers who predestine the destruction of the Truffala forest? Or is it the consumers who demand the products, which producers then eagerly rush to supply? Consumers: that's us, not them.

If we—all of us, not just a few "greedy" corporation executives—did not demand a high volume of petroleum products, for example, the oil companies would not have a market to inspire their relentless search for oil. Please note that many of the modern fabrics and other gear that outdoors people buy in preference to wool are derived from petroleum. Furthermore, do we have to buy the new version year after year?

We should not ask others to adopt our personal spartan buying habits. We both have a bit of Scottish blood in our veins, which we consistently exaggerate, and you know what a Scotsman does with his old razor blades? (He shaves with them.) We don't expect everyone to be as frugal (a five-dollar word for "cheap") as we are. But let us tell you about our windpants.

We had two pair of windpants that had been discarded by two previous owners on the grounds that they were too old, worn, and obsolete. Those windpants became ours in time for the winter season of 1971. They consisted of one piece of ripstop nylon and three elastics. Period. No fly opening, no side vents, no Velcro closures, no zippers, no Gore-Tex, none of a dozen other new special features that make it necessary to discard last year's model for the latest. We wore those windpants from 1971 until 1991, through a lot more winter climbing than most people have time for each winter. The interesting point is that when they finally wore out, the market did not offer any windpants so simple. If we had had the money, we'd have had to buy windpants with half a dozen features we didn't need or want, for a price that amazed us, as we had not looked at windpants prices since 1971. Fortunately, a kind seamstress-hiker friend duplicated the old pair with fresh materials (this time in a softer color, but that's another issue). So now we're set for windpants for the next twenty years.

As with windpants, so with countless other items of outdoor gear. As a group, aren't we climbers (and other outdoor recreationists) "happily" buying too many Thneeds too often? Aren't we supporting a segment of the petroleum industry that, though small, is bigger than it ought to be?

Another classic children's storyteller, George Macdonald, told his little listeners a message their parents might heed: "To have what we want is riches, but to be able to do without is power."

Doubtless you could catch us with frivolous gear among our paraphernalia. We do not dress exclusively in "miff-muffered moof."

What we are saying is that we all should remember: somewhere a Once-ler is cutting a Truffala Tree to supply us with these Thneeds. Don't blame the Once-ler. Look in the mirror. No, wait! Don't buy a mirror! Look in the next clear pool of water you come across.

Take another example. The loggers would not be out there cutting spotted owl habitat if we were not all out here demanding forest products, from planed lumber to wood furniture and houses to the paper that we consume in absurdly wasteful quantities to feed into and out of computers or to produce books that writers like Dr. Seuss and Laura and Guy Waterman feel compelled to write. (We observe that the best-selling books of Dr. Seuss consume a lot more paper than ours.)

Yes, the large corporations do what they can to promote sales through advertising and other marketing tactics. But no one says we, the public, have to go along. It is a point of dispute if advertising can create a demand, as opposed to simply tapping into a latent one. You have to have a lot more faith in the power of advertising than we do, and a lot less confidence in the inherent good sense of people, to believe that advertising controls consumer choice that much. It is a dismal view of the public to say that we do not have the intelligence and the good conscience to adjust our consumption patterns to what are, in the long term, the best interests of the human community and the biosphere on which it rests.

We shall get nowhere in this troubled world as long as we blame our troubles on the tiny minority of corporation executives, whose control over markets is grossly exaggerated, instead of recognizing the responsibility of the entire community to shape its consumption patterns in more environmentally responsible ways. This is one error that the Lorax makes, and so do a lot of the rest of us.

It may seem politically difficult to discipline the thinking and consequent consumption habits of an entire population. Certainly the oil industry doesn't sink or swim on the tiny outdoor-gear segment of its enormous markets.

But strike closer to home—as Dr. Seuss relentlessly does. Those who perceive the problem and are roused to do something about it bear a special responsibility. They are the ones who can rouse public consciousness, initiate the needed dialogue, and argue in the public debate for a more rational policy in the long-term, balanced best interests of all concerned. It is they who can speak for the trees.

In Dr. Seuss's morality play, the Lorax represents that voice. The Lorax is aroused, eloquent, fearless, on the job. But he loses. Why?

Sure, part of the blame rests properly with the Once-ler. We certainly should not let the producers or the corporation executives entirely off the hook. We have to reach them with the message. But that is just what the Lorax signally fails to do. Is it not part of the Lorax's responsibility to find out how to reach them? Is it enough to confront the Once-ler, to shout at him, to marshal the evidence, to predict consequences? To judge by the results, it is not enough. The Lorax loses.

Look at his tactics. When he first appears, he is described as shortish, oldish, brownish, and mossy, with a voice that is sharpish and bossy. He presents facts to the Once-ler; he shows him the consequences of his production methods. But he is bossy. He is shrill, angry, and unconcerned with the Once-ler's objectives and viewpoint. He does not discuss; he issues demands.

One of the most pointed passages in the epic is where the Once-ler, hitherto genial and friendly, albeit unresponsive, finally loses his temper and responds in kind to the Lorax's tirades. He hits close to home when he points our that all the Lorax has said amounts to "Bad! Bad! Bad! Bad!" He rises to assert that he has his rights too on this small planet. If the Lorax expresses eloquence to us conservationists, the Once-ler's aroused cry in this passage surely must appear as eloquence to the loggers, the corporation executives, and—most significant—to the myriads of little people with jobs in the industries of exploitation. With their perspective skewed by self-interest, these folks, these good folks, hear the shrill cries of conservationists as only "Bad! Bad! Bad! Bad!" and they feel that they too have rights as much or more than Brown Bar-ba-loots or Humming-Fish or spotted owls or Alaskan wilderness.

The Lorax loses because he fails to develop an approach that succeeds in reaching either the Once-ler or the Thneed-buying consumers, whose buying decisions support the Once-ler's production operations. At least, even at the height of his fury, the Once-ler has the courtesy to address the Lorax as "Sir," while in his opening words the Lorax tags his opponent contemptuously as "Mister."

What might have worked? A touch of civility perhaps? In American politics of late we've been reaping a whirlwind of invective and extreme accusation. The great Czech leader Vaclav Havel has warned—a warning the Lorax and all of us should heed—"If there is to be a minimum chance of success, there is only one way to strive for decency, reason, responsibility, sincerity, civility, and tolerance: and that is decently, reasonably, responsibly, sincerely, civilly, and tolerantly."

If we fail to see, in our own blighted political landscape, the price of indecency, irresponsibility, insincerity, incivility, and intolerance, at least we can see what it cost the Lorax. Through his communication techniques, he lost.

If those of us who speak for the trees fail in our real world, we should bear as much of the blame as the consumers of Thneeds and the executives of the Once-ler's operations.

It would be easy to be pessimistic in viewing the prospects. Rain forest is disappearing at a frightening daily rate in Latin America; habitat of the last large land mammals on Earth is vanishing in Africa; the Arctic and Antarctic regions are being exploited; world demand for oil and other limited resources keeps "happily" growing beyond all rationality. These trends are destined to continue unless we learn how to reach both the producers and the consumers with the message. Even a contrite Once-ler can see that "UNLESS someone like you cares a whole awful lot, nothing is going to get better. It's not." UNLESS.

Guy Waterman knew he would not be alive when this book was published.

It was characteristic of his life to conceive a project, see it through, then not linger to reap the rewards. He'd be stacking stones for another creative endeavor before the mortar on the last was dry.

His deliberate death by arctic cold on 6 February 2000 on his beloved Franconia Ridge in the White Mountains of New Hampshire caused a seismic reverberation that raced out past our small mountain community into the wide world beyond. I began receiving an outpouring of mail that, as of this writing, hasn't stopped.

Articles immediately began appearing in the press, often speculating on his final choice and both analyzing and eulogizing his varied life as a jazz pianist, homesteader, mountaineer, conservationist, and writer in diverse arenas: politics, business, conservation, mountain history, and baseball.

Guy was sentimental. He relished marking anniversaries of all sorts— one of his more flamboyant, which you read about in these pages, being the sixtieth anniversary climb of Pinnacle Gully. He specialized in taking a situation ripe for disaster—like that Pinnacle climb—and keeping it light-hearted, fun, and instructional.

In fact, in its low-key way, Guy's walk through life was laced with messages. The moral and ethical point lurked never far beneath the surface. Even so, Guy always maintained that nothing in his actions should be taken as example, in particular, our barebones homesteading lifestyle of nearly thirty years. All of us, he believed, should find our own way.

He certainly thought his ending fitted him alone. Above all, Guy stood for the independent responsible choice of the individual.

Even though he didn't linger over them, Guy was good at making the endings. Endings in his hands had style. They never tapered off, slunk un-noticed into the wings, or lost definition. In Guy's grasp the endings were as clear as the beginnings: sharp, crisp, even eager—closing with an excla-mation point or perhaps an indisputable question mark.

So, he orchestrated his own ending.

And it was typical of Guy not to stick around to watch its effects.

In the last months of his life, we worked together as a collaborative team one final time. I was terribly aware of the finality of it as I read his outlines of how we could structure the stories presented here. That was always his strong point: structuring, organizing, and giving meticulous attention to detail. He bounced outlines off me, I reacted, and we discussed; he re-arranged. We performed well together; immediately we were back in the rhythm without missing a beat since our last big writing project together in the early nineties.

We sat facing each other at the wooden table, the surface of which was scarred from our typewriters. This table was where we ate, wrote, read, and shared talk among ourselves and with friends. We scratched out the intro-ductions to each of the pieces, Guy always urging me to choose the ones that most appealed to me. He could complete two drafts to my one, while working as well on transitions, acting as both creator and clean-up man. We'd "exchange papers," as we called it, and pen in a few word changes on each other's work. Guy invariably made tweaks that could heighten the meaning of my sentences and drive my half-thought-out points right into the bone. We both found it an exciting, energizing few weeks. For me, it couldn't last long enough.

He knew he wouldn't be around to see the results or bask in the kudos—if there were any. I was trying to exist in the moment and not think about this enormous thing that was going to happen.

Guy knew he was, like Ahab, going under. He knew—though we never discussed it—that he was leaving me, like Ishmael, to tell the tale.

*Laura Waterman*

15 May 2000

Laura and Guy Waterman have combined writing and mountain climbing for most of their six decades. They met while rock climbing and courted on the rock cliffs of the Hudson and the ice gullies of the Adirondacks. Their wedding night was spent on a small ledge two hundred feet above level ground. Shortly thereafter, Laura and Guy quit their city jobs to move to a remote homestead in Vermont's wooded hills. There, for more than a quarter century, they mixed a primitive, self-sufficient lifestyle with frequent climbing trips and extensive writing about mountain climbing.

It's hard to say which came first, the climbing or the writing. Laura, daughter of a renowned Emily Dickinson scholar, grew up in an atmosphere charged with books and literary creativity and spent summers in the New England hills. She worked as an editor for several New York publishing houses. When *Backpacker* magazine was founded, Laura was its first full-time employee and became associate editor.

Meanwhile Guy, after a fling as a jazz pianist in Washington, D.C., nightclubs, became a legislative aide and speechwriter for well-known Washington political figures, including three U.S. presidents. He later moved to New York City to work as a speechwriter for the top executives at General Electric. However, Guy's boyhood devoted to solitary rambles in the woods ultimately brought him back in his thirties to intensively active rock and ice climbing and New England mountain hiking.

In 1973 Laura and Guy severed connections to the fast track and moved to 27 acres of remote northern Vermont woodlands. Here, they raised their own food, built their own buildings, collected their own firewood, and lived without electricity, plumbing, a telephone, or road access.

In recent years, Laura has devoted her writing talents to fiction, with some fifteen short stories in print. Guy, an occasional short-story writer himself, focused his later efforts on historical research and baseball writing.

*A Fine Kind of Madness: Mountaineering Adventures, Tall and True* draws from the varied writings of Laura and Guy, together and individually, on a spectrum of climbing themes. This collection features both fiction and nonfiction, humor, vitally serious issues, vivid description, and thought-provoking reflection.

---